Friend for Life

The Extraordinary Partnership Between Humans and Dogs

Friend for Life

*The Extraordinary Partnership
Between Humans and Dogs*

Kate Humble

headline

Also by Kate Humble:

Humble by Nature: Life, lambs and a dog called Badger

For Ludo

and these three

who keep me on the right track

First published in 2016
by HEADLINE PUBLISHING GROUP

1

Cataloguing in Publication Data is available from the British Library

Hardback ISBN 978 1 4722 2498 9

Typeset in Bembo by Avon DataSet Ltd, Bidford-on-Avon, Warwickshire

Printed and bound in Great Britain by Clays Ltd, St Ives plc

HEADLINE PUBLISHING GROUP
An Hachette UK Company
Carmelite House
50 Victoria Embankment
London EC4 0DZ

www.headline.co.uk
www.hachette.co.uk

'His name is not Wild Dog any more, but the First Friend, because he will be our friend for always and always and always.'

Rudyard Kipling, 'The Cat That Walked by Himself' from *Just So Stories*

Contents

Introduction
The Big Question

Bella

There is one animal that is familiar to all of us, whoever we are, wherever we live. Even if we've never had direct contact with one, we will have seen one or, at the very least, heard one. For those of us who live in the Western world it is more than likely that one sleeps in our house, possibly even on our bed. I'm talking, of course, of the

I

dog. Yet this animal, which lives alongside five hundred million of us all over the world – as an invaluable partner and a trusted confidant – presents us with one great unsolved mystery: how did this relationship, the most complex and enduring of any between human and animal, start in the first place?

Dogs, scientists generally agree, descended from an ancient ancestor of today's wolves. When dogs became distinct from wolves is not known. What we do know is that some time, tens of thousands of years ago (although we are still unsure as to exactly how many years) something unprecedented happened. Two mammals, both predators, both sharing habitat, both hunting the same prey, each representing a danger to the other, formed an alliance. By this time our ancestors had migrated north from Africa and spread out over the land we now call Europe and Asia. They were hunter-gatherers, living in groups in caves or rudimentary shelters, moving when food sources became scarce. These early humans didn't farm; the idea of agriculture hadn't occurred to anyone yet and wouldn't for another few thousand years. Nor did they keep animals. Domestication of the animals we rely so much on today – cows, sheep, horses, pigs and poultry – was again way off in the distant future. The domestication of those animals seems to make perfect sense. They are good to eat, breed quickly and some can carry more stuff than we can. And yet the very first animal we domesticated, long, long before any other, was one that would just as readily steal our food, or see *us* as its next meal.

Jump forward several thousand years to the present day

and the modern world, with all its whizz-bang technology: its ability to photograph Pluto, transplant hearts and make computers small enough to wear on your wrist. Has the dog, once a valuable aid to ancient humans, become defunct? Not a bit of it. Arguably, the dog is as essential to our survival now as it was to our early ancestors, but in ways that no one could possibly have predicted.

Over the years I've become a bit of an inveterate traveller. My very first foray into lone travel, clutching a Eurorail pass with £100 hidden in a sock in my rucksack at the age of seventeen, prompted what has now been thirty years (God – how does that happen?) of wanderings. I go away for all sorts of reasons. My first trip to Africa was, if I'm honest, a small act of rebellion. I went to Afghanistan in 2009 because I was intrigued and again in 2011 because I loved it so much first time around. I went to Djibouti in East Africa to see whale sharks; Gabon in West Africa in the hope of finding gorillas and surfing hippos; Budapest because I loved the idea of playing chess in a swimming pool (even though I'd long since forgotten how to play). But the journey I'm about to embark on is inspired by our faithful, four-footed friends, that animal that we think we know so well, and one ginger-and-white sheepdog in particular. If you'd like to come along you'd be more than welcome. No leads or poo bags necessary.

Chapter 1
The Dream

Me and Tim with Teg and Taff

If you eliminate smoking and gambling, you will be amazed that almost all an English man's pleasures can be, and mostly are, shared by his dog.

George Bernard Shaw

The four of us waited by Devauden village green looking out for the blue pick-up. It was a surprisingly mild February day so, rather than sit in our truck, we stood outside, shifting from foot to foot, a bit restless and excited. 'That's her!' said Tim and raised his hand as the pick-up swung around in front of us and pulled in.

'Morning!' said Bronwen, as she got out and walked round to open up the back. 'I know you said you wanted a bitch, but I brought one of the dog puppies with me as well, because I just have a feeling, Tim, that you might like him.' She opened the door and we all peered in.

It all started with *One Man and His Dog*. These televised sheepdog trials were watched by millions, and I can't possibly have been the only non-dog-owning, non-sheep-farming person who secretly wished it could be me, standing at the post, dog at heel, its eyes fixed on my face, waiting for the command to send it away up over the hill like an arrow streaking from a bow. I would be glued to the screen, transfixed, following the dog's long, low outrun before a whistle from its handler would bring it to an abrupt halt, flat on the ground, eyeing the small group of sheep which, if everything had gone according to plan, would barely be aware of its presence. Another whistle and the dog would creep forward, low and slow, and if the sheep moved off calmly and slowly in a tightly controlled bunch, it would draw admiration from the commentator. 'Ah, that was a fine lift! Very nicely done indeed. Now let's see how the dog controls them through the gates.' And I would feel my heart-rate quicken as the dog began a sort of dance around the sheep, every whistle or shout from the handler instructing the dog to go this way and that to drive the sheep around the course, through gates, down dips and over rises. 'This bit could give him problems! That's a boggy patch there . . .' By the time the dog had reached the shedding ring my heart would be thudding as if I had kept physical step with every twist, turn and spurt of speed the dog had made.

The shedding ring is an area of the field marked out with piles of sawdust – there is no physical barrier for the sheep to cross. Somehow dog and handler must keep them within the ring and try to split them into two groups. This is fiendishly difficult as sheep like to stick together, and it takes skill, timing and infinite patience to get it right. Frequently a near faultless round will end in disqualification because the time limit set for the course runs out in the shedding ring. Once that task is successfully completed, the final challenge is to pen the sheep in a small, round, gated enclosure. The handler walks to the gate and holds it open, his other arm, crook in hand, spread out as widely as he can stretch. The dog encourages the sheep towards the entrance but it needs to be done by gentle persuasion rather than coercion. If sheep feel rushed or harassed they will just scatter to the four winds. Sometimes they start to go in and my heart lifts, only to plummet again as the last couple baulk at the gateway and bolt. I'm not sure the elation the handler feels at the end of a good round comes anywhere close to the elation I feel on his and the dog's behalf.

I don't know what it was that made *One Man and His Dog* so popular for so many years but, based on my own response to it, I'm willing to guess it was watching an almost magical partnership unfold between man and animal, their apparent understanding of one another and of what needed to be done to complete the task in hand. It is a relationship that is entirely different from one you might have with a pet, or indeed, with any other domesticated animal I can think of. Man and dog are a team and, like watching any great team work together, there is something that inspires admiration and a sort of envy in equal measure. Of course, I might be completely wrong and people watched it because they had a crush on Phil Drabble or later Gus Dermody (there is nothing wrong with having a crush on Gus – I've had one for years), but I'm going to stick to my theory. Something in us, some primeval memory perhaps, is stirred by the sight of man and dog working together, tightknit, success bound up with a deep understanding of their environment and their prey.

Until Ludo, my husband, and I moved from London to Wales in 2007 I had never lived with a dog. When I was growing up my family had a succession of tabby cats, a canary we found in the garden and a series of short-lived goldfish, but never a dog. But despite that, I remember my childhood being very much in the company of dogs because there were plenty around. At the farm next door, where I spent all my time when I wasn't at school or asleep, there were the collies and Paul the farrier's little Jack Russell. Neighbours had family favourites like Labradors and Golden Retrievers. My best friend at school had an Old English Sheepdog, my Japanese godmother a beloved Red Setter called Rupert, and then there was my all-time favourite: Daphne. Daphne was an English Bull Terrier who belonged to the mum of my friend Tris. She bore none of the scars or the bow-legs of Bill Sikes's Bullseye in *Oliver Twist*, but she had every bit as much character and charisma. She could never be described as cute – mercifully – and her robust physique didn't make her very cuddly either, but her unfailingly sweet nature coupled with the rather doleful, ugly beauty typical of her breed made her very much my top dog. On the wall, just above where I'm sitting now, hangs a print by an artist called Ray Richardson. I've had it for many years and I treasure it. It is a slim landscape image of a boy, an airborne football and dominating the foreground the unmistakable profile of an English Bull Terrier. It is dynamic and joyful, always makes me smile and brings back fond recollections of the magnificent Daphne. It is entitled 'Everything's Fine'.

It was a different sort of terrier that I might have brought home as my first dog, had I been allowed. During the mid-Nineties I worked as an assistant producer on an enormously popular BBC television programme called *Animal Hospital*, which told the behind-the-scenes stories of a Royal Society for the Prevention of Cruelty to Animals (RSPCA) veterinary centre in north London. Many of the dogs that came through the door were there for routine procedures. I became adept at spotting a flea allergy or a blocked anal gland from across the waiting room and brutally crossed them off the list of possible subjects to film. A blocked anal gland has little appeal either in real life or filmed in glorious close-up and shown on prime-time telly while viewers are tucking into their shepherd's pie. What the producers were looking for were stories of triumph over adversity, ideally featuring an animal that scored highly on the cute-ometer.

Sometimes we went out with RSPCA officers to attend

rescues. On one memorable occasion I accompanied an officer to a crack den in a block of flats in Hackney. We climbed the concrete staircase and rang the doorbell. The door was opened on to a dimly lit room, curtains drawn against the daylight, someone, deathly pale, lying limply on the sofa. Other people slouched or milled about in the shadows. A man with the wrung-out, wasted look of someone who might have just been disinterred crossed the room with the dog beside him. It was a Staffordshire Bull Terrier, that looked a great deal healthier than any other living thing in the room despite the fact that it had a machete firmly wedged in its skull. The producers decided this was not a story suitable for family viewing.

An equally heart-rending but rather more palatable story that did make the cut was the case of a tiny Jack Russell puppy that had had its tail docked by its owner with a pair of shears. This horrible act had been reported, the dog had been taken into safe keeping and the owner charged with cruelty. The injury was nasty – the stump of the tail bone was exposed and poked out through the wound – but there wasn't lots of blood or pus or innards on view that would clash unpleasantly with the eating of dinner, and it was a story that would give the vet the opportunity to talk about the contentious subject of docking. The final clincher, which made this one of the top stories of the series, was that the puppy was quite the most adorable, wriggly, joyful little thing. Everyone believed she would win the nation's hearts. And she did. She also won mine. At the start of every day I would accompany the vet on duty on the ward round. I would see what cases had been brought in overnight and check up on cases we had previously filmed to see if there was anything we needed to follow up. Our little tail-less star was being kept in until her wound had completely healed and then she would be offered for re-homing. Every morning I would open her cage, which was at chest height, and she would leap into my arms, her bandaged stump wagging with delight.

'Can't I take her home?' I pleaded with the RSPCA officer, but he was resolute.

'Don't be ridiculous, you can't have a dog.'

And he was, of course, right. I lived in a small London house with a tiny yard and, like my husband, worked long hours and was often away, sometimes at very short notice. It wouldn't be much of a life for a dog. I put her back in her cage, hardened my heart and walked away.

A decade later I was back at an RSPCA centre, but this one was in Newport, South Wales. We had moved from Shepherds Bush to shepherding country – a four-acre smallholding in the Wye Valley, surrounded by fields and woods and no road for a mile or more in any direction. Dog heaven. Having passed the home inspection, signed on with a local vet and been introduced to Georgia, the finest and most energetic dog walker in the whole of Wales, Ludo and I were allowed back to the centre to choose our dog. Among the inevitable parade of Staffies and Rottweilers was a little black-and-white mongrel that looked like a cartoon that had been brought to life. As if to make sure we didn't miss him as we walked past, he bounced up and down repeatedly, all four feet leaving the ground, ears flying, eyes pleading. He was scrawny and scruffy, had been horribly neglected, and once taken out of the kennel stood shyly and sorrowfully, refusing to make eye-contact and not wanting to be stroked or petted in any way.

We were unanimous. 'This is the one!' and I discovered, for the first time, the wonderful bond that can grow between a person and their dog, unlike any you can have with your neighbour's dog, or a cat, and especially a goldfish.

Badger, as we called him, became the third member of our household. If we went out, he came too. If we went on holiday it was to places that were happy to accept dogs. We had other dogs to stay to see if he would enjoy the company. He didn't. We taught him how to jump stiles and play Frisbee, which became his favourite game. We discovered that he has a peculiar obsession with feet and socks, likes stinky cheese and crunching ice cubes and that he is scared of almost every other living thing, including pigeons and rabbits. We also discovered that nothing and no one welcomes you home with quite such an unadulterated display of sheer delight than your dog, that they have an unfailing ability to make you laugh, that you become convinced they can understand everything you say and that however vociferously you think otherwise they will always end up sleeping on your bed, even if it is just an occasional treat . . .

Two years later, perhaps like parents who decide it would be good for their only child to have a sibling, we thought Badger might be ready for a companion. We sought advice and chose carefully. Bella, another rescued mongrel, but this time from a less traumatic background, seemed to fit the bill perfectly. Smaller and younger than Badger, we thought that would still allow him to feel like the alpha dog, but as she was infinitely less needy he wouldn't have all the attention taken away from him. Our efforts were not appreciated. Badger took one look at Bella and decided that the best way to deal with her was to pretend she didn't exist. Which takes some doing. Small she may be, but she looks like a cross between a warthog and a hyena, walks like a muscle-bound prizefighter and sports an extremely splendid Mohican the length of her back, which has prompted complete strangers to ask which dog groomer we take her to. Over the five years they have been together they have worked things out to live in a strange sort of harmony. No sharing beds, or any sort of touching; the Frisbee can be shared, but there is a special system that must be adhered to; Badger gets first dibs at the front seat of the car; Badger drops a couple of biscuits outside his bowl when he is eating and leaves them for Bella to clear up. Badger goes to Ludo if he needs reassurance or a bit of attention. Bella will go to anyone, particularly if they happen to be holding a sausage sandwich.

It wasn't just dogs that came into our lives when we moved to Wales. As we had bought a smallholding it seemed necessary we populate it with the sort of animals smallholders have. So we started with chickens and geese and ducks, graduated on to pigs and donkeys, and eventually, when we felt a bit more confident and I had had several months as a trainee shepherd in preparation for the TV series *Lambing Live*, half a dozen Badger Face Welsh

Mountain ewes, which I intended to breed. Neither Badger nor Bella took any interest in the other animals and showed no inclination to chase or round anything up, which for the most part was a very good thing. We share a boundary with a much bigger farm that raises both sheep and cattle, and the last thing we wanted was a constant concern that our dogs might be heading off through the fence to worry our neighbour's livestock. However, there was one memorable morning when I longed with all my heart to have a dog that was a bit more practical.

It was coming into May and all the ewes – my flock had swelled to the heady total of ten – had lambed in March. It is this time of year that I usually really enjoy. The worries and sleep-interrupted nights of lambing are over, the weather is warm, the days getting longer, the ewes are getting plump on new spring grass and the lambs are at their most playful and endearing. For no discernible reason they will sometimes gather together and then chase around the field in a gang, leaping and bouncing, literally, it appears, brimming over with the joys of spring. But the May of 2012 was as wet and cold as the April preceding it. The fields were a quagmire, the sheep muddy and plagued with foot rot and I was living in soggy, smelly Gore-Tex that never got a chance to dry properly. Having animals – dogs included – means that there is no retreating under the duvet hoping the rain will stop. Dogs need exercise, livestock need feeding and checking. It was while I was checking the ewes and lambs on a particularly foul morning that I noticed something amiss with one of the lambs. She was a ewe lamb – a lovely 'single' that had grown beautifully without a twin to compete with. Seemingly oblivious to the downpour, the lambs were chasing each other across the slope of the field but I noticed that this one was finding it hard to keep up, despite being one of the biggest, and her breathing seemed laboured. I needed to bring her and her mother into the shed to see if I could find out what was wrong.

The field they were in is about two acres in size and slopes steeply down from where the sheds are to woods at the bottom. Had it been the winter, all I would have had to do was stand at the top, shake a bucket of sheep nuts, and they would all have come running. But this was spring. Sheep nuts hold little allure when there is lots of fresh grass about and I didn't have any anyway. In vain hope I got a bucket and rattled it with no success. I then spent the next hour slipping and sliding in the mud, rain hammering down on my head and into my eyes trying desperately to herd the sheep into the yard adjoining the shed. They were having none of it, and even the sick lamb proved impossible to catch. In despair I sat in the mud, put my head in my hands and wept. If only, I said to myself, if only I had a sheepdog.

Ludo had made it quite clear that as far as animals were concerned we had quite enough. There would be no more, not even dogs. And of course it was ridiculous to seriously contemplate having a sheepdog when we only had a handful of sheep. And although I can do a very passable whistle through my fingers, I'm not sure any sheepdog would have the slightest idea what I was whistling about. So, somewhat regretfully, I dismissed the idea of having my own dog, but instead wondered if anyone would teach me how to work with a dog, if only to fulfil my *One Man and His Dog* fantasy.

Humble by Nature is a rural skills centre that Ludo and I run on a farm a few miles from home where we work in partnership with farmer Tim Stephens. Tim and his wife Sarah live on site and keep two hundred Welsh ewes and a herd of Hereford cattle on the land. They also have two cats, called Pickle and Beetroot, and a bewildering collection of dogs – some pets, some working and some ageing, much-loved retirees.

I've heard many farmers claim that it is only possible to have one perfect dog during your working life, and Tim and Sarah both agree that no dog they have ever had has come close to competing with Wig. Widget – or Wig for short – was a dark Blue Merle working sheepdog with one blue eye and one brown eye. Over tea after we had done the morning's feeding and mucking out, they told me about him.

'We bred him,' said Sarah, 'but he wasn't any particular breed.'

'He was so clever!' added Tim. 'I was shearing a farmer's sheep near Malvern and by mistake I let an unshorn ewe out of the shearing trailer into the field with the already shorn sheep. Wig went into the field and rounded up and caught that particular ewe, in among all the others, and brought her back. If a lamb was born at night out in the fields he could always find the mother.'

Sarah reminded Tim that Wig had also been responsible for him finally fixing the door of his Land Rover. 'It had been broken for months,' said Sarah, 'and I had almost fallen out so many times, but Tim only got round to fixing it after it flew open and Wig fell out.'

'Well, Wig couldn't hold it shut!' retorted Tim.

Contrary to the idea that all working dogs sleep outside in kennels whatever the weather, Wig slept firmly under Tim and Sarah's bed. Wig died at home at the remarkable age of seventeen and was replaced by his son Dai – a sweet-natured, solidly built dog who is loyal, faithful and willing, but, Tim admits, not the quickest dog, either physically or mentally. 'He's never really come close to working like his dad.'

I asked if Tim would be willing to teach me how to work with a dog, and whether he thought Dai would take commands from anyone other than him.

'I've got another idea,' he replied. 'I've been thinking for a while now that I ought to get a young dog to train up who could eventually replace Dai. How about we share one and we can train it and work it together?'

It was a perfect plan but swiftly went awry that day in Devauden as soon as Bronwen opened the back door of her pick-up. In the back was Bronwen's bitch Missy, a perky, copper-coloured dog with pricked ears and startling blue eyes. I'd never seen anything like her.

'She looks like a little fox, doesn't she?' said Bronwen. She sat serene and apparently oblivious to the mayhem going on in the straw at her feet. Seven puppies squeaked and played and jumped on each other, chewing tails and ears, snarling, yapping and rolling about. Tim, as Bronwen predicted, was immediately drawn to the dog pup. Solid and strong, bright-eyed and alert, he was unashamedly handsome, with white chest and muzzle, but his coat was predominantly a deep rusty red.

'These are Welsh sheepdogs,' Bronwen explained to me. 'They're a bit different from collies and you often get this red coat colour. That dog pup looks just like the father. A really good dog he is.'

In the meantime Sarah had picked up another of the pups. She looked a bit like Missy, with her rich copper-and-white coat, but she had the most mesmerising eyes — one half blue and half brown and the other with a sort of white star across the pupil. She sat in Sarah's arms looking down her long nose with bewitching effect. I looked across at Tim holding the dog puppy and knew he'd found the one he wanted. I looked again at the puppy in Sarah's arms and knew she was the one for me.

Ludo guessed what was coming. 'We're not having another dog,' he said firmly.

'But she won't be at home,' I pointed out. 'She'll live at the farm and she'll be a working dog, not a pet.'

'You have no idea how to work a dog.'

'I'll learn.'

Chapter 2
The Reality

Adeline and Smasher

In order to really enjoy a dog, one doesn't merely try to train him to be semi-human. The point of it is to open oneself to the possibility of being partly dog.

Edward Hoagland, American author and essayist

A friend of ours had a dog called Trousers. A splendid name until you have to shout it across a hillside. Similarly Badger's one and only true love is a whippet called Princess Tallulah Tinkerbell. Again, not overly practical when it comes to giving instruction. There is a good reason why most working dogs have snappy one-syllable names like Tess, Fly or Moss. Tim and I followed tradition. He called his puppy Taff and I named mine Teg, which in the Welsh language means fine or beautiful and seemed to me to be more than fitting. We made them a kennel from a garden shed, which we put in a sheltered corner of a barn. Tim built them a run, I went to the local farm store and bought collars that didn't fit and a bed that their over-eager puppy teeth demolished in a matter of hours. Straw made a much more practical substitute.

In those early days they had two modes of operation: frenetic activity – jumping on each other and anything else they could find, rolling about, scrapping, biting ears and tails, running around in demented circles – and the opposite: total wipeout, when they would collapse and lie like abandoned toys, often one on top of the other, and sleep like the dead.

As they grew, and spring came, we started taking them out into the fields, at first just to scamper and play, but it wasn't long before I was taking them around the entire four-kilometre perimeter of the farm and they would cross the fields full tilt, always competing and trying to outpace each other. They were mesmerising to watch, and although both were still a little clumsy and not entirely in control of their limbs – particularly Teg who was swiftly beginning to resemble a gangly teenager with overly large feet – their strength, athleticism and stamina were already coming to the fore. It struck me then that I had taken on an animal that was an entirely different beast from my small, grateful, rescue mongrel from Newport. This was an animal with an identity, a purpose and huge, as yet untapped, potential. This was not a dog that was going to thrive on a gentle saunter around the local woods and then contentedly spend the rest of the day upside-down in a basket next to the range in the kitchen. Even when she was just a few months old it was blindingly obvious that my puppy was not a pet. She had the brain, physique and energy of an animal bred to work. She was the direct descendant of working stock and I realised that for her to be truly content she needed to be allowed to fulfil the role she had been bred for. The weight of responsibility hit me full force in the stomach.

Some months before I got Teg we had been asked if we would rent a couple of acres of our farmland to a retired teacher called Lois who lived down the road in our local town of Monmouth. She had long harboured ambitions to compete in sheepdog trials, despite never having farmed or owned sheep. Perhaps *One Man and His Dog* had had the same effect on her as it did on me. Anyway, Lois set about achieving her wish by buying a young collie and finding a trainer to teach her and the dog the rudiments of sheep-dog trialling. She bought half a dozen sheep with which to practise and a lorry-load of hurdles which, with Tim's help, she set up in a wide circle in one of our fields. She would drive her sheep into the hurdle enclosure and then work the dog around the outside to help it learn the commands and understand the way the sheep responded. The sheep could see the dog and would react to it, and the dog could obviously see the sheep but wasn't actually in direct contact with them. This struck me as a very good way to go about things.

Taff and Teg were six months old and Tim had started to let them in with some of his sheep. We worked them separately but, nonetheless, the result was never anything other than sheer, unadulterated chaos.

'Oh God,' I muttered, my hands covering my face. I peeped horrified through my fingers to see Teg, a blur of ginger and white, race around and through the sheep like it was the best game ever. She'd split one off from the rest then chase it down, snapping at its hindquarters, my increasingly desperate calls of 'That'll do' falling on entirely deaf ears. The only shred of comfort I could take from this was that Tim fared no better with Taff, who if anything was even more wild.

'At least we know they're keen!' said Tim with his usual optimism. 'There are some sheepdogs that for whatever reason just don't work, they don't "see" the sheep and no amount of training will help. Our two have all the right instincts. We just need to work on them so they are doing what we want them to do, rather than what they want to do.'

I looked down at Teg, who was lying in the grass, sides heaving from her exertions, tongue lolling. If you'll excuse a little anthropomorphism here, she appeared to be smiling. If a dog can be euphoric she was showing all the signs of being exactly that. This, her great, grinning, panting face seemed to say, was what I was born to do.

I tried working Teg using Lois's hurdle system and had a modicum of success. She learnt quickly, picking up the commands 'Away' to send her around the sheep in an anticlockwise direction, and 'Come by' to send her the other way, although I often got confused and told her the wrong thing. But what became increasingly obvious was that my total lack of experience meant we couldn't progress much further than we'd got, and I couldn't expect Tim to be available every time I wanted to work with Teg. There was another issue too, which Sarah brought up. Littermates kept together can result in all sorts of problems. It's known as 'littermate syndrome'. Sometimes the symptoms are so mild as to be barely noticeable, but with some dogs it can lead to constant fighting, separation anxiety and even aggression towards their owner. 'It might be best if we separate them,' she said.

My reaction to this idea was twofold. Part of me was delighted. Although I'm at the farm whenever I'm not doing another job, there will be weeks when I don't get there at all. This had no effect on Teg, who still got fed, walked and endless attention, but, selfishly, I felt I missed out. I missed out on seeing her first thing in the morning and last thing at night. If she was at home, I realised, I could walk her before I set off to work and if I got back in daylight I could work her with my few sheep. I would be able to spend more time with her and allow the bond that at the moment she had with her brother to be with me. She wouldn't be alone all day, because she would go with Ludo and the other dogs to the farm and I would still get to practise with more sheep in bigger fields when Tim was around.

The other part of me was nervous. This was exactly the outcome Ludo had feared would happen: that we would end up with three dogs at home which he'd have to deal with when I went away filming. We wouldn't need to buy a kennel – we had a stable Teg could sleep in – but I knew she was just one more responsibility on top of all the other animals that he had to look after when I was away, and I feared he would not be over-enthusiastic about the prospect.

In the end it turned out that as usual he was way ahead of me. He had predicted that this was on the cards and was already resigned to the idea of her living with us. So one autumn afternoon I lifted Teg into the back of our truck and took her home. That night was the first one she had ever spent away from her brother, the first in all the eight months of her life she had ever spent entirely alone. I lay awake, listening to her plaintive howls and whimpers echoing across the garden, and had to use every shred of willpower not to get up and go to her. Eventually silence fell and I got off to an uneasy sleep, only to wake at dawn. I dressed hurriedly and ran through the paddock to her stable. I peered over the door to see my beautiful dog, curled up in the straw, fast asleep. As I was gazing at her like an adoring parent, she opened one eye and gave me a look as if to say, 'Good God! What are you doing up at this ridiculous hour of the morning?'

With Teg at home and conscious that she needed loads

of exercise, I got into the habit of getting up early and walking or running for an hour or so before breakfast with all three dogs. Badger, as usual, was unconcerned by the presence of a large, bouncy adolescent because he just ignored her. Teg seemed to understand almost immediately that Badger is a law unto himself and is best left to get on with his own devices. And anyway, she had Bella, small, brown and belligerent, to torment and tease into finally losing her temper and chasing Teg, teeth bared, growling with frustration, as Teg danced about just out of her reach. Teg learnt from the other dogs how to jump stiles, how to sit and wait before crossing a lane and would even make tentative attempts to swim if we were by the river. Up at the farm Badger and Bella would contentedly sleep under a desk in the office and Teg would lie just as contentedly in the yard. In short, she seemed to have taken to her new role as part pet, part working dog with no problems at all. She seemed to genuinely relish being around people, she was getting plenty of exercise and occasional working sessions with the sheep, but still I worried. I worried that I would somehow spoil her and her chances of ever fulfilling her working heritage if I didn't get some help. I needed to find someone nearby who could train me and help me train my dog. I sent an email to the enquiries page of the Welsh Sheepdog Society website entitled 'a young dog and a first time owner' asking for advice. A reply came back that same day.

To begin with, where do you live? You really need
somebody to mentor you who has used Welsh Sheepdogs

before, rather than a Border Collie trainer, as they are different kettles of fish when it comes to training! Let me know your stamping ground and I'll try to hook you up with a local who can help.
Adeline

I'm near Monmouth, in Monmouthshire.
Kate

Am I near enough at Tenbury Wells? I don't claim to be the hottest shot but my dogs all work for me and my senior dog has worked open hill and as a demo dog at the NSA 2013 Welsh Sheep event. He'll do a pen, load a trailer or a race, work 500 sheep or one sheep or cattle, split them, so he has most of the necessary. I do sometimes help people start them. Depends what you want out of your dog really, I want them to work without much direction as my hands are always full of drenching kit or whatever, so what I do is try and get them as much as possible to read the situation and my body and work off that, though of course you have to have words of command too for when it's not clear or their idea of what is happening is different from yours! If you want very precise stuff to put him on a fag packet in the middle of a bracken patch, I'm not your gal.
Ad

I would love to bring Teg up to you and for you to see what you make of her. I do harbour a small desire to do trials, but that might be utterly unrealistic. I just want to

make sure I don't spoil or waste a dog with good potential,
if that makes sense.
Best wishes
Kate

I too have a sneaking desire to take a Welsh dog to a trial,
but close, tight work isn't really their forte – Border
Collies have been bred for years to accept micro-
management from their handler, Welsh dogs have been
bred to work independently and some of them really
resent this type of handling and will quit if subjected to it.
I'm around Thursday or Friday if you want to bring Teg
up then.
Ad

'Right, Teg,' I said, as I opened the door of the truck and
she jumped in, 'this is a big day. I'll do my best not to let
you down, but try not to let me down either.' In response I
got a particularly disdainful look down her nose before she
stretched her lanky length out on the back seat and went to
sleep. By the time we got to the gate of Adeline's farm I
was jittery with nerves. Throughout the hour or so it took
to get there I had worked up a scenario in my head that
now seemed so realistic I almost turned heel and fled. My
biggest fear was that Adeline would pronounce Teg ruined,
untrainable, not fit or reliable enough to work; that she
would say, 'It's a shame because she is clearly a good dog,
but you just left it too late.'

I drove through a field of sheep and over a cattle grid to
the big old red brick farmhouse. Leaving Teg in the truck,

I walked to the front door. Wellies were strewn around the step and unseen dogs barked from the barn the other side of the hedge. The door was open, revealing a dimly lit hallway. I called 'Hello?' and a tall, dark-haired woman appeared in a well-worn fleece, muddy jeans and baggy socks. I felt immediate kinship. 'Come in and we'll have a coffee before we start.'

I liked Adeline instantly, and not just because of our shared fashion sense. Forthright, down to earth and honest, Adeline by her own admission doesn't do niceties and claims she is rather better with animals than she is with people. Originally from Mid Wales, where her mother bred goats, Adeline moved to her husband Tim's family farm when they married. They have five hundred breeding ewes but Adeline's real passion, apart from her dogs, is for horses. She breeds Quarterbacks and before we took the dogs out she took me to see some of her youngsters. They were magnificent animals – like paintings by Stubbs or Whistler brought to life – but what left a greater impression on me was the way Adeline was with her animals. It is hard to pinpoint, but she radiates a sort of calm, quiet authority that comes, I suspect, from having a really deep understanding of animal behaviour learnt, not from books, but from patient hours of working alongside them.

I went to fetch Teg. 'She's a good-looking animal,' said Adeline. (My heart did a small leap of pride.) 'Do you know what her breeding is? It would be nice to get her registered if we can.' I told her and she knew of the father, but didn't know about Bronwen's Missy.

'I'll get in touch with her and find out. Now, let's go and get Smasher.'

Smasher is Adeline's senior dog. He couldn't look more different to Teg. He has a broad head with a blunt snout, his body is much chunkier and thicker set and, instead of Teg's copper-and-white colouring, he is black and white with a wonderfully distinct face – half black and half white. We walked them together to a field that had about eighty of Adeline's ewes in. 'Keep Teg on the lead and ask her to sit,' said Adeline. Mercifully, Teg did what she was told straightaway. So far, so good. Then I stood, increasingly open-mouthed as I watched Adeline work with Smasher. She gave him the command 'AWAAAY!' and he ran out to the right of the sheep and got behind them. Then he drove the sheep towards us, constantly running in an arc behind them to keep them together. He didn't crouch or crawl like a collie, but stood tall, head and tail both up, nor did he fix the sheep with that classic collie stare. In fact he barely seemed to be looking at them at all. He didn't push the sheep too hard but kept them moving at a steady, even pace up the field, keeping them together, but not uncomfortably tightly bunched. When they got to within about ten feet of us he stopped. So did the sheep. He stood behind them, occasionally shifting position slightly if one of the sheep showed signs of breaking rank. Apart from the initial command to send Smasher away, Adeline hadn't said a word. She hadn't whistled, gestured, anything.

'Bloody hell!' I said admiringly.

'So now,' she said as we approached the sheep, 'I can check them over or catch one and Smasher will keep them together for me, and if I want to move them, say from one field to another, I can walk ahead of them and Smasher will keep driving them to me.' And I watched as Smasher did exactly that, again with no command.

'That'll do, Smasher,' she said and he returned to her side and the sheep wandered off back into the field.

'That was just beautiful to watch!' I said, trying hard not to think of the uncontrolled chaos that ensued anytime Teg was allowed to work sheep. And it had demonstrated what Adeline had told me about the way Welsh sheepdogs work in contrast to collies.

'It is actually the main criteria we use when registering them,' said Adeline. 'As you can see with Smasher and Teg, Welsh dogs vary enormously in size, colour, shape. They are not easy to categorise in the way other breeds are, but it is the way they work that defines them. Now, why don't we see how Teg does?'

My nerves came rushing back with a sickening lurch. 'Are you absolutely sure? I don't want her to damage your sheep. She's pretty wild and she's not great at coming back once she's started.'

'We'll send her out with Smasher. Don't worry about the sheep. They can look after themselves.'

I unclipped Teg's lead. Adeline sent Smasher away and a beat later I gave Teg the command. She needed no further encouragement. 'Let's just watch what she does,' said Adeline and we did and this time I didn't cover my eyes with my hands. I could see her taking her cues from Smasher, she emulated the arc he ran to keep the sheep together. Occasionally she would come too far round and the sheep would turn or straggle away and Smasher would bring them back into line and keep driving them towards us. Although not quite as neatly done as when Smasher was working alone, Teg had, to my inexpert eyes, at least, done pretty well. I looked anxiously at Adeline.

'Well, that was pretty good, don't you think?' she said.

'To be honest,' I laughed, 'I'm absolutely stunned.'

'They often work well with another dog when they are learning. Call her off them now and let's see if she'll come.'

'That'll do, Teg,' I called and my brilliant, angelic dog walked away from the sheep and came straight back to me. We walked towards the house, our dogs to heel, and me feeling on top of the world, when suddenly Teg turned on her heels and was racing back towards the sheep.

'THAT'LL DO!' I yelled at the top of my voice. 'TEG!!!! THAT'LL DO!' She didn't falter, didn't pause, I might as well have just remained silent.

'Let's see what she does,' said Adeline, unfazed. 'This'll be interesting.'

I thought mortifying might be a more appropriate word, but I said nothing and watched, every nerve tense. Teg ran round the back of the sheep, got them together and then ran back and forth to drive them towards us. I laughed in sheer disbelief. 'She's a clever dog!' said Adeline. 'I think we can do something with her. The first challenge is going to be stopping her working!'

I drove home elated. I hadn't ruined my dog – not only that, she had shown real promise and suddenly my dream of that partnership, the extraordinary bond that seems to exist between humans and dogs more than with any other animal, felt within reach. And that bond seems all the more extraordinary and all the more special because of its unlikely origins. How did Teg's wolf ancestors and my ancient human ancestors ever come together in the first place? And how did wolves transform from fearsome predators to become our best, most faithful friend? The more I thought about it, the more I wanted to find out, but at that moment had no idea what a surprising and fascinating journey lay ahead.

Chapter 3
How Did It Start?

Russian scientist Dmitry Belyaev and silver foxes

Ever consider what our dogs must think of us? I mean, here we come, back from the grocery store with the most amazing haul – chicken, pork, half a cow. They must think we are the greatest hunters on earth.

Anne Tyler, American author, in *The Accidental Tourist*

The beginning, according to *The Sound of Music*, is a very good place to start, but, it turned out in this case, not a very easy one. I trawled the internet, turned to well-known authorities on dogs – Bruce Fogle, Ray Coppinger, Stanley Coren to name a few – but it soon became apparent that no one yet has found a definitive answer to when or how humans and wolves began the association that was to have such a profound and long-lasting effect on both species. Any information I was going to get would be a matter of guesswork. All I had to do was find a person well qualified to make as informed a guess as possible. As Director of the Palaeogenomics and Bio-Archaeology Research Network in the Department of Archaeology at Oxford University, Greger Larson fitted the bill. I got the train.

I used to live in Oxford in my late teens. I'd done my A levels, left school and announced to my parents that I was finished with education. This wasn't what they had in mind for me at all, so a compromise was proposed. I would do a three-month secretarial course and after that I was free to do whatever I wanted. The course was at a college in Oxford. I suspect this wasn't a random choice. It wasn't close enough to home that I could commute in to class every day and it would mean I would have to lodge with a local family. I think my parents hoped that being based in a famous university town would give me a taste for academic life. It didn't. Instead I met a South African girl on my course whose descriptions of her home country made me want, more than anything, to go to Africa. So, when I finished the course, I rented a store room, just big enough to fit a single mattress on the floor, in a student house on the Botley Road for the princely sum of £20 a week, bills included, and stayed in Oxford for another nine months working in offices during the day and pubs at nights and weekends to earn my airfare.

It felt rather nostalgic returning now, more than twenty years later, to a town that was familiar enough that I recognised bits of it, but not enough to find my way to Little Clarendon Street without making a couple of wrong turns. It didn't matter; I was early and it was a beautiful spring morning. The trees were in blossom, bluebells crowded the flower beds of front gardens and a blackbird gave melodious accompaniment to the soft squish of sensible academic shoes on the pavement and the clunk and squeak of well-used, heavy-framed bicycles.

I met Greger in his rather sparse corner office and was almost immediately ushered downstairs to the café below, where he clearly does most of his work. I will confess now that I have met and interviewed Greger before for a TV programme and developed somewhat of a professional crush on him. He is one of life's great enthusiasts, endlessly curious, talks at a rate of knots, knows more about Pearl Jam than perhaps even Pearl Jam does and renders useless any carefully prepared list of questions because his conversation always inspires further inquiry and before you know it you've been talking for four hours on a range of topics far wider than you ever intended. Settled in with a large flat white, he asked where I wanted to begin. I had just read a book by an American professor, Pat Shipman, called *The Invaders* with the strapline 'How Humans and their Dogs Drove Neanderthals to Extinction', which is the sort of strapline that a clever publisher clearly thought would make anyone want to buy the book. It certainly

35

worked for me. However, within its own pages Shipman writes that Neanderthals were extinct by the time wolf-dogs appeared, which made something of a nonsense of the strapline, but I was intrigued by the thought that Homo sapiens and Neanderthals might have coexisted.

'Oh, without question,' said Greger. 'Not only that, they shagged. Neanderthal DNA is in all non-Africans today.' And only after a fascinating hour or so later, when we had discussed early human migrations, climate change, hunting techniques, mitochondrial DNA and more evidence of different hominids having sex did I get around to asking Greger about the skull of a Palaeolithic dog that had been discovered in Goyet cave in Belgium. It is believed to date from 32–36,000 years ago, and although it differs from a wolf skull, it is also different from a modern-day dog skull. But was it proof that the domestication of wolves was already far enough advanced to have changed the skull shape of the animal? Greger took another hit of his flat white.

'I think it's open to interpretation. Rather than just assume that it's a dog, I think that there are three or four other things that it could very easily be, and until we eliminate those possibilities I'm not comfortable jumping to the conclusion it must be a dog.' He then went on to explain that thirty thousand years ago there was a whole range of animals that looked virtually identical, but pursued very different behavioural niches or dietary niches and that led to changes in their physiognomy. The Goyet skull might well have been one from a wolf that had adapted to its particular niche and environment. 'Just because it superficially resembles some of the characteristics that we associate with the differences between dogs and wolves, doesn't mean it was a dog. We don't know whether, thirty thousand years ago, wolves behaved differently depending on the habitat they lived in, or whether some wolves differed physically or genetically from others. It could very well be that changes in teeth and skull shape overall was something to do with the fact that you had wolf lineages that were specialising in hunting megafauna – animals like mammoths – or in some other niche. These changes might have had nothing whatsoever to do with domestication.'

The prevailing hypothesis according to Greger is that real evidence of changes associated with domestication came much later – about fifteen thousand years ago. 'But, *could* the domestication process have started before then?' I queried.

He nodded. 'But what I don't know is how long it was before that, because you have to have some way of noticing the differences in the archaeological record. It could very well have been that there were lots of relationships and processes that were taking place that were leading to that point but are invisible to us because the changes aren't yet on the skeleton itself. What I don't know is how long a period of time it takes a population of wolves to follow people around before you end up with this kind of physical change. It could be very, very, very slow, over tens of thousands of years, before you end up with what we recognise as a dog. But,' he added, 'why did people domesticate wolves?'

'Well, I was just going to . . .'

'And to me that's the wrong question.' I hastily shut up. 'When you're talking about early domestication what that pre-assumes is that there was an intentionality about it, that people saw an opportunity and then went for it. But what opportunity was there? I've stayed in places where there are wolves wandering around, they're scary, they wanna eat you, they're much more powerful than you are, why would you wanna bring them in to your social circle? That begs the question, why the hell did it happen? Why would early humans choose to do it? At this point nothing has been domesticated. We don't have plants, we don't have animals. There's nothing with floppy ears, a shortened face and that barks and yaps and is cute with an upturned tail and will run around and play ball. There's nothing to tell us this would be a good thing to do, so you have to come up with a scenario that is plausible evolutionarily that doesn't require human intentionality.'

The most obvious theory that I could come up with was that wolves would choose to follow our early ancestors for the same reason that fox populations have grown exponentially in our towns and cities today: access to food. The bones and other scraps that we threw out made an easy feast for wolves brave enough to hang around in our vicinity. Greger agreed that was almost certainly the case, but it begged another bigger question. How, over time, did these wolves start to change genetically and become distinct from other wild wolf populations? His theory is that the wolves which exploited the niche of following humans gradually started to differentiate from other wild wolf populations; they fed themselves on human leftovers, they developed a shorter fight or flight distance, and those behavioural differences saw an increasingly marked physical split from other wild wolf populations, which over time became a genetic split as they came into contact with each other less and less. Not only that, but the wolves following humans would have had a vested interest in keeping other wolf packs at bay. They didn't want any competitors for the resources they were successfully exploiting, so it is likely they would have started to act as sentinels – guards against other marauding packs – with an unintentional but nonetheless obvious benefit to the humans they were living alongside.

'So,' I asked tentatively, 'is it too far-fetched to say that what was evolving was a symbiotic relationship between humans and canines?'

Greger shook his head between mouthfuls of sandwich. We had moved on now from flat whites to lunch, the tables around us had filled up, conversation was loud and lively, as was the coffee machine. 'There will have been some sort of mutual way that both humans and wolves were benefiting from the other that entrenched the relationship and then allowed for subsequent selection. Gradually the difference in behaviour and looks between wolves that followed humans and the wolves that did not would have become more and more apparent with each generation. Wolves were effectively domesticating themselves.'

So although we still don't know how long ago wolves became dogs, the theory Greger had outlined as to how the unlikely partnership between wolves and humans might have started, appears very feasible. I can't of course, make a direct comparison, living as I do in a country that eradicated its wolves long before I was born, but if we look at foxes as our nearest equivalent it is very easy to see how different fox populations have learnt to exploit their own niches, and how they behave around humans as a result. In the Welsh countryside, where I live, it is rare to see a fox, despite the fact that I live on the edge of a wood, stuffed full of the sort of small animals foxes love to eat and plenty of places to hide. And that is precisely why I hardly ever get more than a fleeting glimpse of them. They don't need me. They have all the resources to survive without having to fraternise with humans. By contrast, while filming at Kew Gardens in London over the best part of a year, we were regularly visited by a fox which would hang around the vegetable garden with a hopeful expression. Although it hadn't quite lost all its inhibitions – it remained just out of touching distance – it was utterly at ease around us and had clearly developed a taste for sandwiches. And muffins. In common with so many urban foxes it was exploiting a niche which meant where it slept, what it ate, how it behaved was entirely different from its country cousin.

But the other question that arises here is, why would wolves have changed into the vast array of shapes, sizes, colours and characteristics that we see in dogs today? Well, the answer is that at some point we did start to interfere and we did start to breed selectively. Initially it would presumably have been for practical reasons – dogs to guard us, dogs to hunt with. It was only later that we started to selectively breed animals that would be nice to kids, not leave hair all over the house or be amenable to being carried around in a handbag. But many of the physical attributes we associate with dogs are common across the species, whatever their breeding. Badger, Bella and Teg all look very different. Bella is small and stocky with a predominantly brown coat and a white flash down her chest. Badger is taller, but more wiry. He is black and white and his coat is longer and silkier than Bella's. Teg is bigger than both of them – roughly twice Badger's size and weight – and her coat and colouring are different again, but all of them have ears that flop down and tails that curl up. If you have a dog, I'm willing to bet a Bonio that it too has ears that point down and a tail that points up. A long-running experiment that has been going on in a distant part of Siberia can shed light on to why that is.

If you have read many dog books – and I have – you will certainly have come across the story of a remarkable scientist called Dmitry Belyaev, so apologies if I'm telling you a tale you already know. Belyaev was born in Russia probably in 1917, although details of his early life are sketchy. His family were peasant farmers but they also understood the value of education. Their eldest son left the family farm and became a scientist specialising in genetics. In his early teens Dmitry was sent to live with him in Moscow to continue his education. This was at a time when Stalin was in power and convinced that every level of society was infested by spies and corruption. Hundreds of thousands of people were sent to gulags in Siberia or just shot without trial, including Dmitry's older brother. Being a scientist was not a safe occupation and certainly not one working in genetics, which Stalin viewed as contentious and subversive. In 1948 geneticists were declared enemies of the state, genetic institutions closed down and any reference to genetics in text books was eradicated. At this time Belyaev was working at the Department of Fur Animal Breeding at the Central Research Laboratory in Moscow. His work was predominantly with Silver Foxes – much prized for their fur and the more silver the fur, the more valuable it was. He was a strong believer in Gregor Mendel's laws of inheritance. Back in the mid-nineteenth century Mendel had done experiments with pea plants which led him to come up with the theory that certain 'factors' like the colour of his pea plant flowers were passed on to the next generation. What he'd hit on was genetics, but no one took much notice of him or his ideas until he was long since dead. His theory was 'rediscovered' at the beginning of the twentieth century and a whole new area of science was born. Despite the fact that in Stalinist Russia practising this science would lead to certain death, Belyaev published a paper on 'The variation and inheritance of silver-coloured fur in silver-black foxes'. He was sacked, but curiously allowed to live and continue working, albeit in a godfor-saken corner of Siberia. And it was here that he made a ground-breaking discovery that many view as the key to explaining how wolves became dogs.

The foxes he continued to work with had all been bred and raised in captivity but they were still wild animals. Most would retreat to the back of their cages snarling and spitting when a human came near, but some did the opposite and would approach the bars rather than shy away. It was these 'tamer' animals that Belyaev chose to breed to see if tameness was a genetic trait that would be passed down the generations. And if so, was there some sort of link between selectively breeding for tameness and changes in anatomy and physiology akin to those seen between wolves and dogs?

The results were astonishing, not least because the changes in the foxes' behaviour, physiology and anatomy happened incredibly quickly. Within just six generations some of the cubs of these carefully controlled matings wouldn't just allow themselves to be approached by people and petted, they, like dogs, actively sought out human contact. Their adrenal glands – which control the fight or flight reflex – were smaller and the levels of blood cortisol that increase with stress were lower. Within forty-five generations the foxes had changed so much they could be mistaken for a different species entirely. They had developed smaller skulls and canine teeth. Their coats were splotchy and their tails were curled – all common physical attributes of a domesticated canid. In short, Belyaev's tame wild foxes were wild no more. He had domesticated them. He'd turned them into something more like a dog.

There is somewhere rather more accessible than Siberia where it is possible to fully appreciate the difference that domestication has made and see what makes dogs dogs and wolves wolves. It's called the Wolf Science Center and it's near Vienna. I had read about it and was intrigued by the work they were doing there, so sent an email to one of its founders, Professor Kurt Kotrschal, with a list of questions. I received a reply a few days later. 'A comprehensive reply to this would blow the frame of this mail,' he wrote. 'Real new insight came via the recent results from the Wolf Science Center and also the Clever Dog Lab. Maybe plan a visit?'

I needed no further encouragement and the following week I took a plane to Austria's capital city. Professor Kotrschal was away, but before he left, he'd put me in touch with Karin Bayer, the manager at the Clever Dog Lab. The lab was founded by Dr Zsófia Virányi, Priv.-Doz. Friederike Range and Professor Ludwig Huber and is part of the Messerli Research Institute based at the University of Veterinary Medicine. Thanks to meticulous directions and Vienna's wildly efficient public transport, I arrived at the green gates rather too early and had to walk around the perimeter of the campus until it was time for my meeting. The security guard on the gate pointed me in the direction of the right building but in a complex of almost identical buildings I found myself dithering on the path, unable to read the German signs and wondering if he meant the building on the right or the building on the left. Happily I was waylaid by a petite woman in the company of a large, shaggy German Shepherd.

'Are you Kate?' she asked, surprisingly, and in perfect English. 'I'm Rachel. I'm doing a PhD here. I'll take you up and introduce you to Karin.'

The Clever Dog Lab attracts students from all over the world. Although dogs have lived alongside humans for many thousands of years, it seems that it is only in the last thirty or so years that they have become the focus of rigorous and wide-ranging scientific research. Karin showed me a complex experiment being undertaken by a

44

student from South Korea who was trying to ascertain how dogs use their eyes to communicate. I met a student from Nepal who was studying cognitive ageing in dogs. I was introduced to the dog Michel, who belongs to one of Karin's colleagues, and gave me a tireless demonstration on a touch-screen computer of a dog's ability to read human emotions from facial expressions.

'Apart from using your colleague's dog, where do all the dogs come from that you work with here?' I asked Karin.

'They are pets,' she told me. 'We asked dog owners in the area if they would like their dog to take part in some of our research and we had hundreds of people come forward. They come together to the lab and the dogs have a lovely time – lots of attention, training and rewards. It is something different for them.'

Rachel appeared, large dog still at her side. 'Come and see what Akina's been up to!' I followed her into a large white room. There were cameras in all the corners, markings on the floor and in the middle two wire mesh enclosures side by side, with a sliding gate between them. Rachel explained that her PhD was looking at altruistic behaviours like giving, helping and sharing in wolves and dogs, whether they show them and to what extent. 'We have the opportunity here to work with pet dogs, the dogs at the Wolf Science Center that have been raised exactly the same as the wolves, and the wolves themselves, so we can make a really nice comparison across all three groups.'

Wolves, she explained, have to cooperate in their daily lives. They live as a pack, they hunt as a pack, they breed as a pack, so it makes sense that they would have these kind of tolerant, prosocial tendencies towards each other. But what she is trying to find out is how much domestication might have affected a dog's prosocial tendencies and whether a dog would be more willing to show prosocial behaviour towards a human than another dog.

I couldn't even begin to imagine how she would be able to ascertain such a thing. She laughed. 'We have lots of fun coming up with ingenious ways to test theories and a very useful team who can build things for us! Come on, Akina, let's show her what you can do.'

The experiment was simple, but ingenious. Akina was put in one of the mesh enclosures, with the gate left open to the second enclosure. In front of her was a board with two symbols on it – a yellow star and a black cross. She had been trained by Rachel to touch the symbols with her nose, but touching only the black cross would give her food. The food is delivered to the second pen and during the training session she is allowed to go and claim her reward. The real test comes when another dog is put in the adjoining pen. How long would Akina keep doing the test to see another dog get the reward, and would it make a difference if it was a dog she was familiar with rather than a dog she didn't know?

Rachel was keen to stress that the experiment is ongoing but early results show that dogs will continue working longer for dogs they know than they will for an empty cage next door and no reward. But for dogs they don't know, they will work an even shorter time – to use Rachel's words they appear to make an 'active decision to stop working'. Early tests involving humans are giving indications of other surprising results. A dog is given the same test – to touch a symbol – but in the cage next door is either a person they know or a complete stranger. I imagined that a dog might work for the familiar person and not for the stranger but, so far, it seems dogs aren't motivated to see humans rewarded for their efforts. As Rachel's colleague Mylène told me, 'They stop working very quickly and it makes no difference whether or not it is a person they are familiar with. But what is funny, is that if they touch the right symbol and don't get rewarded, they will bark and beg towards the person they know, but not with someone they don't.'

It was fascinating stuff, and revealing too, but it didn't really give me a sense of how much domestication might have affected not just the physical appearance of dogs, but the way they behave and think. Rachel smiled. 'That's what we are all trying to find out, but if you come to the Wolf Science Center tomorrow we can show you what we are working on. I'll be there late morning, but Friederike says if you can get there at about 9am you can go for a walk with a wolf . . .'

Chapter 4
Wolves In Dogs' Clothing?

Friederike and Aragon

Slowly, deliberately, the dog turned from the black wolf and walked towards the man. He was a dog and dogs chose men.

Jim Kjelgaard, American author, in *Snow Dog*

The Wolf Science Center is forty or so kilometres north of Vienna and in the grounds of a wildlife park. Thanks once again to Austria's enviably efficient public transport, my country bus, which I shared with a small gaggle of hearty, chatty ladies in floral dresses and a silent man munching his way through a large meaty sandwich, dropped me as the timetable said it would, at precisely three minutes to nine, outside the gate. It was a rather grey, cold Saturday morning, despite the fact it was August, and the wildlife park was deserted. At the kiosk selling tickets and ice creams, a woman pointed me along a track and I followed it, past little paddocks with goats and sheep and then out into the park where deer grazed under the trees, barely bothering to lift their heads as I passed. After about ten minutes I came to a building behind a high wire fence and a sign declaring that this was the Wolf Science Center. I pushed open the gate and walked in. There seemed to be no one about, so I walked around until I saw a figure through the window. She came to meet me at the door.

'I've come to meet Friederike,' I explained.

'She's running a bit late, but do go and walk around and see the wolves and dogs. She should be here in about twenty minutes.'

The last time I'd been in close proximity to a wolf had been two years before. I never actually saw the animal itself, but I did witness first hand the conflict between wolves and humans that has ultimately led to their demise. I spent a few weeks living alongside a family of nomadic herders in Mongolia's Southern Gobi Desert. Their yurt, or *ger* as it is known there, was pitched in a river valley, two thousand metres above sea level, surrounded by a vast expanse of rugged, mountainous pasture. I camped just down the valley from them, but spent my days helping with the sheep and goats. There are no fields or boundaries, the animals graze out on the open hill, but always accompanied by someone from the family on their horse, and three stumpy-legged dogs that were a lot more athletic than their looks gave them credit for. At night, the flock was driven back to the *ger* and corralled in a stone enclosure to protect them from large predators like snow leopards and wolves which, given the opportunity, will take advantage of easy prey.

Not long after I arrived in the valley, I was asked to go and help round up the horses. The horses were pretty much left to their own devices, being far better able to defend themselves than sheep and goats, but in the early spring the foals are starting to be born and the family drive the herd down to pastures closer to the *ger*. It was an unforgettable, glorious experience to be out in that immense landscape galloping along in the wake of a herd of wild horses, flying hooves kicking up clouds of dust. We drove them to the pasture behind the *ger* and then one of the men, Batsok, expertly lassoed a mare who had already had her foal. Together we caught the foal, and checked it and the mother over before letting them loose. 'That's the first one of the year,' said Batsok. 'She's a good one.'

That night I crawled into my tent and fell asleep instantly, exhausted by the day's exertions. The dogs' barking woke me. When you live alongside dogs it becomes relatively easy to recognise different barks – I can certainly tell when Badger and Bella are barking because my husband has come home or when they are barking because a stranger has arrived. These Mongolian dogs were barking with an urgency and ferocity which was completely uncharacteristic. I switched on my torch. It was four o'clock in the morning, pitch dark and bitterly cold. I should get up, I thought. A wolf might have come down to the corral. But then I realised I was scared. I had never seen a wild wolf before, had no idea whether venturing out into the dark armed with only a penknife and a head torch would save the sheep or whether I was putting myself in a position where my hosts would find my mauled corpse on their doorstep in the morning. So I took the cowardly option and stayed in my sleeping bag. The dogs stopped barking and I drifted back to sleep.

Batsok was already up and saddling his horse as I approached the *ger* in the early dawn light. 'The dogs were really barking last night,' I said. 'Has anything happened?'

Batsok looked grim-faced. 'Yes. I heard them too, but I didn't get up. I should have. A wolf came and killed the foal.'

The impression we are given of them from a very young age is that wolves are the baddies of the animal kingdom. Think Three Little Pigs or Little Red Riding Hood, and it is easy to see why the wolf has an image problem. But the wolf that killed the foal wasn't bad, or evil, it was simply doing what predators do to survive. The wolves at the Wolf Science Center may have had human contact, be 'tamed' to a certain extent, but they were still wild animals with all their predatory instincts intact. I approached their enclosure with a degree of trepidation, unsure whether I would be acknowledged, ignored or eyed up as potential breakfast.

The enclosure was quite large and wooded. At first I couldn't see any wolves at all but then I spotted two grey shapes in the shadow of the trees. If they had noticed me they didn't show it. Then, suddenly, silently, another wolf appeared walking along the fence line towards me. It was a huge creature, with an immense head and a black coat. I wouldn't have been surprised if it had red eyes, but of course it didn't. The eyes, that gave me the most cursory of glances before it walked on without breaking step, were amber.

A volley of barking told me, even before I could see them, that I was nearing the dog enclosures. I was intrigued to see these dogs that were living outside as part of a pack. How would they react to humans? Would they be fearful, friendly or non-committal? Like the wolves they had all been hand-reared in peer groups until they were weaned and then put with other dogs of different ages to live in a pack, but their reaction to me as I approached the fence couldn't have been more different. They stood on their hind legs, paws against the wire, barking. Not aggressive 'Go away or I'll rip you to bits' barks, but 'Hello! hello! I'm over here!' barks. Even to the casual observer the way the wolves had reacted to me compared with the dogs was markedly different. Whereas the wolves appeared to shun any human interaction, these dogs were begging for it.

Old dog training methods, now largely and mercifully rejected, encouraged owners to think of their dogs as wolves trapped in a dog's body, and the way to train them was to behave like the alpha animal and treat our dogs as subordinates. But as esteemed biologist, dog breeder and trainer Raymond Coppinger puts it in his pithy book on the subject, 'Dogs can't think like wolves, because they do not have wolf brains. We descended from apes, but we don't behave like them and we don't think like they do. We are a much different animal than the apes in spite of our common genetic ancestry. The same is true of the dog and its ancestor.'

I'm writing in the kitchen and all three of my dogs are here too. Bella is lying spread-eagled on the sofa, Badger is curled up in a ball with his bum firmly against the range and Teg is lying half in and half out of a basket, snoring like a drunken man asleep on his back. It is hard to credit they have a shred of wolf ancestry at all. Domestication has clearly had a profound effect on dogs but just how profound is what the scientists at the Wolf Science Center want to find out.

I returned to the centre and as I did so I saw a woman in a red jacket standing right up against the fence of the wolf enclosure, the big black wolf I had seen earlier standing directly opposite her. It wasn't jumping up with its paws against the fence but it was displaying signs that it was definitely delighted to see her. She turned and held out her hand. 'Hello. I'm Friederike Range.'

Friederike is a German biologist. After doing her PhD with primates and how they use cooperation, she wanted to take her research further. As she put it, 'One animal that cooperates quite a lot and quite intensely is the wolf.' In 2008 she co-founded the Wolf Science Center with Professor Kotrschal and Hungarian scientist Zsófia Virányi. Together with Zsófia she had already established the Clever

Dog Lab but they wanted to broaden their area of study and explore not just the human–animal relationship but also the animal–animal relationship. They believed that to have a better understanding of why dogs cooperate with us, communicate with us and are attentive to us, they needed to be able to study how wolves interacted with each other and how they learned from each other. Not only that, they wanted to make a direct comparison with dogs to try and establish what traits may have been lost or exacerbated by domestication. To do that, they needed both sets of animals to be raised and treated in exactly the same way. Studying wolves kept in zoos and comparing them with pet dogs was never going to give clear scientific results.

They got their first project funding at the end of 2008 and since then have undertaken research on a wide range of subjects – difference in tolerance, aggression, social learning, gaze-following abilities to name a few. To enable these studies to happen requires both dogs and wolves to be sufficiently comfortable around humans to allow them to be trained, and motivated enough – usually by food – to do a task again and again. But the wolves I had seen didn't appear to be tame at all, until Friederike let the big black one out of the enclosure and put it on a lead.

'This is Aragon,' she said. 'He will take a while to get used to you and you need to let it be his choice. Just be calm and quiet and if he comes up to you, don't lean over him and put your face close to his. Let's go this way.' And she plunged off in the rain, pushing her way through the sodden vegetation, Aragon on a long lead choosing his own path. Occasionally Friederike would call, 'Tree! Tree!'

when Aragon's lead got wrapped around a trunk, and Aragon would retrace his steps. He took no notice of me at all. I felt rather hurt.

After about half an hour we came to a clearing in the woods and Friederike thought Aragon might be ready to meet me. At her suggestion I sat in the wet grass and waited for the wolf to approach.

'Hold out your hand!' Aragon gave it a cursory sniff and was rewarded with a treat from Friederike's pocket. We hung about a bit longer, but he remained largely uninterested, and although it was somewhat thrilling to be in close proximity to such an impressive animal, ultimately it was a rather underwhelming experience because there was no connection. It made me realise how important the interaction we get from our dogs is to our relationship. I love being greeted when I get home by three wagging tails and three sets of pleading eyes vying for attention. We love dogs because they appear to love us.

Back at base, Friederike showed me a video of an experiment they had set up to compare cooperation and tolerance between animals of the same pack. The clever props department had built a table with a sliding top. On it was placed a tasty snack, but to bring it in reach the animals needed to pull a rope to slide the top towards them. However, the rope is attached to the table top in such a way that if only one animal pulls one end of it, it won't move. To get the food, the animals need to cooperate and each pull one end of the rope at the same time. I watched as Aragon and a subordinate female wolf were released from a pen. Together they raced across the enclosure towards the table. Both animals seized an end of the rope at the same time and got their food reward. This, explained Friederike, is unsurprising.

'Wolves are dependent on cooperating and on tolerance within their group. They will be very aggressive towards animals that are not part of their pack, but within a pack they will cooperate with any animal, whatever its ranking.'

And what about the dogs? Contrary to what I thought, they demonstrated rather less tolerance and willingness to cooperate than wolves. Watching two dogs do exactly the same experiment was fascinating. Like the wolves they raced across the enclosure but, as they neared the table, one, the female, hung back, apparently intimidated, allowing the male dog to grab the rope, but of course failing to get the food. But when the same experiment had been conducted before, researchers found that the dogs could be trained to cooperate and successfully complete the task, but only with a great deal of human input. Other problem-solving experiments have revealed the same pattern. Put food into a container that requires some persistence to get it and wolves will keep trying until they succeed. Dogs will try for a bit and then look hopefully at a human for help. Domestication along with selective breeding appears to have diminished in dogs the ability to learn insightfully that wolves have, and although that might sound like a bad thing, it actually means our partnership with our dogs can be more successful because we have more influence over them.

I watched another test between the wolves and the pack dogs that demonstrated this all too clearly. One of the trainers stood in a room with food on a chair beside her. Her task was to prevent the dog and then the wolf from getting near the food. She could use gestures and her voice but have no physical contact with the animal. A handler came in with a dog and let it go. Immediately the trainer near the food started yelling, waving her arms, trying to block access to the food with her body. The dog took a tentative step towards the food and then thought better of it, retreated behind the legs of the person who had brought it in and then tried to get out. In total contrast the wolf, instead of being inhibited by the trainer yelling and waving, stood its ground and persisted and persisted until it got the food. But interestingly it didn't bite. It showed no signs of aggression. As Friederike pointed out, 'Wolves are very good at restraining themselves with people they know. That relationship matters. It would be different with a stranger as they are very afraid of people, but if they build up a good relationship they are not going to do anything to jeopardise that relationship without needing to.'

Which perhaps gives some insight into the very early relationship between our ancient ancestors and wolves. To Friederike, the alliance between wolves and humans makes perfect sense. 'The domestication of wolves happened before the advent of agriculture, so there would have been no competition or threat to humans. Wolves wouldn't have been killing livestock, there would have been sufficient prey for both humans and wolves to coexist without competing. But wolves have many of the traits that we look for in our dogs. They are highly social, highly cooperative, highly socially attentive, and highly tolerant.'

But I was interested to know why the dog in that experiment had reacted so differently; had been so apparently intimidated when the wolf hadn't been at all. Why had the dog reacted that way? Was it a direct result of the domestication process? Friederike was cautious. 'That's what we assume. That's our hypothesis but, again, I have to be careful because we haven't published that yet. But it makes sense that at some point humans would have selected animals that didn't show any aggression or were easily inhibited from doing so. We don't want an animal in our home that is going to be constantly trying things out. I don't want to be challenged by my dog every time I go to the fridge!'

So have we dumbed down our dogs? Wolves, it seems, when set a problem, will tend to work it out, whereas dogs will often give up and look to a human for help. Does that make wolves smarter than dogs? Not necessarily. As Friederike says, you could argue that dogs are actually smarter because they will turn to humans to solve the problem for them! And although Friederike and her colleagues have had great success training wolves to do certain things, there are some things that a dog will do that a wolf won't. As Raymond Coppinger points out, 'People can train lions, tigers and leopards to jump through flaming hoops, but with all the interest in wolves, why hasn't anyone taught a wolf to sit on a chair with a wolf biscuit perched on its nose?'

A Swedish wolf biologist called Erik Zimen had the notion to form a dog-sledge team entirely of wolves. He spent a long, cold winter trying to get them to accept the harness, the weight of the sledge and to travel in a straight line. It was a disaster. They ignored all commands, got hopelessly tangled up and ended up getting increasingly aggressive towards each other until finally a monumental fight broke out. Dogs, as Friederike put it, are incredibly intelligent animals, just in a different way. They pay attention to exactly the right things – give us what we want and make sure we don't want to be without it. 'A dog gives us the feeling that we are the most important people in the world. Every dog owner who comes home will feel loved. There's someone waiting there who, no matter how late you are, no matter what might have happened before, is always completely happy to see you.'

And that is undeniably true. It is one of the great joys of having dogs. Even coming down to the kitchen first thing in the morning elicits a volley of joyful barks, licks and general wagginess. If I go away for weeks, the welcome is even more ecstatic, particularly from Bella, who runs around in circles like a demented warthog and then pees, copiously, on the kitchen floor.

The general consensus seems to be that wolves chose to hang around humans, rather than humans actively going out, finding wolf cubs and taming them. But those early humans didn't put up with the wolves because they gave them an ecstatic welcome every time they returned to their cave or shelter. What early humans saw was that there was an advantage to having these animals on their side. The wolves offered them protection, albeit unwittingly, by keeping at bay other predators that wanted to compete for the food humans provided. Millennia later the domesticated descendants of wolves – dogs – still haven't been surpassed by anything else in their role of guards and protectors. There is a lovely story of a Yorkshire Terrier called Joe that was published in an American magazine in 2013. Joe lived with his owner Deborah in New Jersey and one warm summer day, Deborah heard Joe barking in a way that alerted her something was wrong. A fully grown adult black bear had walked through the open back door of her house and was heading for Joe's food bowl. Joe launched an attack which, against all odds, worked. His frenzied barks, growls and nips drove the bear away. His food was safe and so was Deborah. In a house in Pompeii is an incredibly detailed, almost lifesize mosaic from the first century AD. It depicts a dog, crouched as if to spring to the attack, its teeth bared, straining against the chain attached to its red collar. Beneath it are the words 'Cave Canem'. Beware of the Dog. Many a garden gate today bears the same sign, sometimes alongside a snarling image of a fearsome-looking Rottweiler. The police, security firms, the army all use guard dogs. Very quickly we realised that a four-legged animal, which was smart, territorial and social, was definitely a useful asset to have around. What none of our early ancestors would have predicted is just how useful they would become.

Chapter 5
I'll Scratch Your Back...

Simon Mogford, Tango and Safn y Coed Fly

A shepherd may be a very able, trusty and good
shepherd . . . But what is he without his dog?

James Hogg, Scottish poet and novelist,
known as 'The Ettrick Shepherd'

I drove along the Heads of the Valleys road. It was still early and a low mist hung over the hills and fields like dry ice. Although the trees were still heavily hung with leaves, the air was chilly and felt distinctly autumnal. I turned off, somewhere south of the Brecon Beacons, on to a narrower road and wound my way down a series of lanes, which soon became more rutted, with grass pushing through the tarmac. A final, steep climb up a track so narrow the car was brushing the hedge on either side and I reached a farm. As I got out of the car, I set off a cacophony of barking from the row of kennels outside the farmhouse. A man appeared from behind a Land Rover wearing a tweed cap and checked shirt with two more dogs at his heels. I shook hands and introduced myself, feeling a bit like a citizen of Lilliput meeting Gulliver. Simon Mogford is a man of stature: tall, bearded and, it seemed entirely feasible to imagine, broad enough to withstand a charge from the entire Welsh rugby team. Adeline had told me that Simon is one of the most respected trainers in the Welsh Sheepdog Society and it is his skill as a handler that has made him invaluable to Operation Mint Sauce.

Operation Mint Sauce may sound like a Comic Strip spoof, but it is a serious response to a serious problem. Much of the land in the vicinity of Simon's farm belongs to the Forestry Commission, and there are conifer plant-ations interspersed with areas that have been felled and replanted almost as far as the eye can see. Over the years, sheep from some of the neighbouring farms in the area have taken advantage of poorly maintained fences and escaped. Nigh on impossible to find in the dense forestry, the escapees generally remained at large, and they thrived. Welsh sheep are hardy and resourceful. There's plenty of shelter in the plantations when the weather turns bad, water from the many streams and certainly no shortage of food. Not only could they survive with no problem at all, so could their offspring. The runaways started breeding with each other and before long there was a population of well over a thousand feral sheep that had never had any contact with people, wandering over a huge area. Does it matter? you may ask. Well, it does if you have spent considerable time and resources planting new trees to replace the ones that have been harvested. Sheep like nothing more than a tasty sapling and new plantations were regularly being decimated by these ovine outcasts. Like the sheriff's office in a Wild West movie, the Forestry Commission offered a reward to anyone who could catch the sheep, and Simon was one who took up the challenge.

He introduced me to the two dogs he had with him. Jack had red-brown shaggy fur, kind eyes and a laid-back demeanour. 'He may seem very quiet and relaxed, but he's a good worker. Got a tremendous bark on him. All the litters he's fathered have produced good barkers.' Barking is an important attribute of the Welsh dog and one of the things the society looks for when assessing dogs for the purposes of registration. Simon's other dog couldn't have looked more different. Smooth-coated, black and white, he had the appearance of the sort of perky little mongrel a rescue centre might use on a campaign poster.

'Is he Welsh?' I asked.

'As Welsh as Welsh can be,' said Simon. 'His name is

Tango. I'll be working with him today. He's the best of my dogs with the feral sheep.'

When I had arranged to come and meet Simon, I had asked if it would be appropriate for me to bring Teg, but, he told me, the work was too dangerous for a young, inexperienced dog. 'There are some big cliffs and drop-offs out there. You can't have a dog that is too keen, gets carried away and won't listen. You need to be confident you can stop her or she and the sheep could end up going over the edge.' Far from confident that I could either stop her or tell her to go in the right direction, I heeded Simon's advice and left Teg at home.

I climbed into Simon's Land Rover, heaving up with me a basket laden with flasks of tea, ham rolls and Welsh cakes made by Simon's wife Emma in anticipation of a very long day. Tango jumped in the back, Simon hitched up a trailer and we set off. We made our way down the hill, through the old mining village of Treherbert in the bottom of the valley and then climbed again, winding up and up, and at every turn the views got grander and more majestic, a vast expanse of peaks and saddles, woodland and heath.

'And somewhere out there are the sheep you've got to catch?!' I said to Simon in amazement.

He nodded. 'They have their habits. We have a pretty good idea where to look and if Tango picks up a scent, he usually finds them.'

We drove through a forestry gate and along one of the gravel access roads to a bend where Simon pulled up. 'It's a sunny day,' he said, 'and they'll often come out and graze where the sun is. You see that slope over there?'

he said, gesturing with his crook. 'The sun will hit that in the next hour and I wouldn't be surprised if that's where we find them. We'll take a walk and see if we can pick up any tracks.'

I walk a lot. Not only do I get great pleasure from it, but having three active dogs means that I have to get out every day and in every sort of weather. I am used to scrambling through woods, puffing up hills and picking my way across pretty rough ground, but I struggled to keep up with Simon. He set off down the track, crook in hand and Tango trotting along beside him. 'There are some tracks there,' he said, pointing at the rough tussocky grass, and plunged off down the hill, oblivious to the piles of rotting brash left when the area had been felled and was now well disguised by thick grass.

'There are more here!' he called, but I was too far behind, stumbling and cursing, my feet breaking through the rotting wood and plunging me into holes up to my knees. 'How the bloody hell does he do it?' I muttered. Finally I caught up with him. The tracks he pointed out had been all but invisible to me, but here was evidence even I could see. Patches of grass were flattened and there were scatterings of sheep dung about. 'They were lying here, probably last night,' said Simon. 'You can see the track they used to make their way here. I think they probably headed down and over that stream. We'll go back up to the forestry track and work our way round from there. It's a bit easier going.'

Simon has caught over a thousand sheep since Operation Mint Sauce was started in 2008, and he and Tango seem to have developed a sort of sixth sense, an acute awareness of these sheep and their behaviour. The early autumn and winter are the times when it is easiest to track them down. There is less vegetation about, making the sheep easier to spot, but it is also the time when the ewes come into season and the rams will seek them out. And it was a little group of ewes, with a couple of ram lambs and one big mature ram, all horns and balls, that Simon and Tango spotted, not out on the open hill but in a dense plantation of young trees. The trees hadn't yet been thinned out, so the trunks were barely a metre apart. Narrow shafts of sunlight penetrated through to the forest floor, which was carpeted in a thick, moss-covered layer of brash and brambles. Tango trotted over it all with his customary delicacy, weaving his way through the trees, appearing not to be really paying any attention to the sheep and yet, as if he had cast some spell over them, they gathered up into a tight group and stayed put. Tango continued to wander nonchalantly around, sniffing at something or other, lifting his leg, but if one of the sheep gave the slightest indication that it might take a chance and bolt, Tango was instantly back on full alert. What was interesting was he kept his distance from the sheep, he worked very quietly, not panicking them, but leaving them with no doubts at all of who was in charge.

'This is why a Welsh dog is perfect for this work,' explained Simon. 'A Border Collie works low to the ground, with its eyes fixed on the sheep. In a wood like this they would very quickly get injured because they would be too intent on concentrating on the sheep and not looking at the obstacles around them. And you notice that when Tango feels the sheep are under control he relaxes. He knows he doesn't need to keep worrying about them and that means he conserves his energy. We can be out for hours some days and he never tires.'

And with that, Simon walked into the group of sheep and, before they were really aware what was happening, he had grabbed one, turned it on its back, tied its back legs together to one of its forelegs, and flipped it back so it was lying on its belly on the ground. It took a matter of seconds and looked deceptively easy, but I knew what I was witnessing was a hugely well-honed partnership between man and dog that was a result of a deep understanding born out of many years of experience.

'What are you going to do with them now?' I asked, when the final sheep was trussed up.

'Carry them out to the trailer,' said Simon, and with that he hoisted the ram, which must have weighed something in the region of seventy or eighty kilos, on to his shoulder and strode off through the trees. 'I ought to help,' I thought, and chose the smallest of the ram lambs. 'Bloody hell,' I said as I tried to heave the bemused animal off the ground. Even the little ones were fat and strong after a summer of good grass. By the time Simon returned I was still struggling.

'Bring the head up to your knees so it is sitting on its haunches,' he showed me, 'then put your arms around its belly and as you lift it turn it so it can sit on your shoulder, leaving one arm free. That way you can use your stick to keep your balance.' And in one balletic movement, he had swung another animal up on to his back as if it weighed no more than a sack of hay. I suddenly had a vivid reminder of the Asterix cartoons I loved as a child, with Simon and Tango perfectly cast as Obelix, Asterix's enormous friend with superhuman strength, and his tiny, much-loved black-and-white dog Dogmatix.

I looked down at the lamb at my feet, and he returned my look with one of bored contempt. 'Right,' I said, 'this can't be that hard,' and I manoeuvred him into the position Simon had showed me, bent down to circle his belly with my arms and heaved with all my might. I managed to lift him somewhere in the region of my waist, but there was absolutely no way I could see of getting him any higher, and certainly not up on to my shoulder. I became overcome with helpless giggles and staggered out of the woods, hauling my contemptuous lamb with me in the same time it took Simon to carry out two more.

'What happens to them now?' I asked, as we closed up the trailer. Simon poured tea into mugs and I wiped sheep poo off my hands on to my jeans, before accepting one of the finest Welsh cakes I have ever eaten.

'All these sheep will have been born out here,' said Simon, between mouthfuls. 'They won't belong to anyone, so they go to market to be sold. The proceeds go to the Air Ambulance. The Air Ambulance has done a lot to help farmers over the years. This is a way of giving something back.'

The day had been something of a masterclass. It had shown me not just what a Welsh sheepdog is capable of but also just how much Teg and I had to learn. As I drove back, slightly sleepy after a day of fresh air and too many Welsh cakes, hoping Liza Tarbuck on the radio would keep me awake, I tried to work out what it was that so struck me about the way Simon and Tango worked together. I realised that Tango, for the most part, had appeared to work without commands or instruction. His training, his experience and his trust in Simon allowed him to go about his job pretty much independently. And it was clear that Simon has complete, unwavering confidence in his dog and his abilities. I had witnessed not simply a well-trained dog working faultlessly with a skilled handler, but something beyond that, something more akin to a collaboration, a combining of skills to form a strong and very effective partnership.

But there was something else about that day that gave me an insight into how dogs might first have worked with our ancient ancestors. As Greger pointed out, it is not hard to imagine that humans would put up with the presence of wolves and later their gradually domesticated descendants because their superior sense of smell and hearing would act as an alarm and their physical presence as a deterrent. But at some point dogs went from being handy to have as neighbours to being well and truly part of the family, venerated and adored. We may think it is a modern, First World phenomenon that we are soppy about our dogs, but archaeological evidence indicates we have held these animals in high esteem for a very long time. In Bonn-Oberkassel in Germany an ancient burial site was discovered dating back 14,000 years. In it were two human skeletons, two artefacts made from bone and antlers and the bones of a dog. A grave was excavated in Ain Mallaha in Israel dating back 12,500 years and contained a human skeleton, curled up in a foetal position, with the skeleton of a puppy beside its head.

Greger suggested I get in touch with Angela Perri. Angela is a Postdoctoral Fellow at the Max Planck Institute for Evolutionary Anthropology in Germany. Her PhD thesis 'Hunting Dogs as a Global Foraging Adaptation to Early Holocene Temperate Environments' brings to light evidence of what appears to be a shift in the human–dog relationship, in not one, but three separate parts of the world. We live in the Holocene today – it is the geological epoch that began around 12,000 years ago, when the world started to emerge from the chilly Pleistocene and get warmer. With the changing climate came a change in vegetation and areas that had previously been more tundra-like became forested. Angela looked at three such areas, one in the Southern United States, one in Northern Europe and one in Japan. In every one she identified burial sites; not just of humans, but of dogs. These sites – and she has identified over four hundred of them – revealed remains of dogs that had clearly been buried with care and consideration. The earliest dates from nine thousand years ago but the most startling one she came across was in Skateholm in Sweden. Dating back about seven thousand years, it contains the skeletons of dozens of people buried alongside several dogs. One burial seems to have been undertaken with particular care, the body laid on its side, chips of flint scattered around it, a pair of antlers and a carved stone hammer buried alongside it. And this was the body not of a person, but of a dog. This dog, Angela believes, was given these burial honours because it was much revered as a hunter.

Angela's hypothesis is that dogs gained special status during this period because of the new challenges humans faced hunting in forest rather than open grasslands. But as my whippet-owning friend Kirsty will attest, her dog can pick up a scent and be away long before Kirsty realises that there is a squirrel or a rabbit in the vicinity. Dogs can do some things far better than we can, like follow a scent and run fast over a long distance at the same time. Dogs can flush out prey or retrieve it if it is injured and gone to ground, and those talents would have proved invaluable to our hungry early forest-dwelling ancestors. Being out with Tango gave me an insight into how effective that innate instinct to hunt and chase can be when it is harnessed. Simon and I might have been amply provided with provisions, but if something had happened to cause us to be stranded for longer than the ham sandwiches could have sustained us, I have no doubt that with Tango's help we would have survived very happily on feral lamb.

Burying dogs with prized bones and weapons was one way to show them our gratitude, but it wasn't long before we found another way to immortalise them. Today we dog owners take embarrassing numbers of photos of our dogs with our phones and look at them when we need cheering up. Well, I do anyway. But six thousand years ago, before Steve Jobs had evolved, prehistoric people took to drawing pictures of their dogs on their living-room walls. There is a particularly beautiful example of this in an

Algerian cave deep in the Sahara Desert. The painting shows men hunting oxen with bows and arrows and with them is a dog, nose to the ground, with a curly tail – and now we all know that a curly tail is a sign of domestication.

But then something happened that was to see the status of our canine companions temporarily tumble. About ten thousand years ago, probably in the area known as the Fertile Crescent (in the modern-day Middle East), some communities started cultivating plants and domesticating other animals like sheep and goats. Angela Perri noticed that in many of the places that agriculture started to be taken up, dog burials ceased. Our canine companions, it seemed, were no longer top dog. Dog remains have been found dating from that time, but not as carefully laid-out skeletons. Bones are scattered and bear evidence of being broken or hacked by some sort of weapon. For the early farmers, dogs had become dinner.

But if dogs had been reduced simply to something we ate, I wouldn't be writing this book. Dogs may have been a handy source of food, but, people discovered possibly as far back as eight thousand years ago, they could also be helpful in other ways. Angela found the bones of dogs at a site in Denmark that, she said, indicated 'that they had small, medium and large dogs'. Her theory is that these dogs had been selectively bred for specific tasks. Although she couldn't guess what the small dogs might have been used for (could they have been the first pets?), the medium-sized animals were built like hunting dogs and the larger ones were almost certainly used as pack animals. When the Chiribaya people were living in Southern Peru over a thousand years ago, dogs were once again being venerated, but not as hunters. Now there were other domesticated animals, humans had found another way of using dogs: to protect their livestock. The Chiribaya were llama herders who valued their dogs so highly they were buried in human cemeteries, wrapped in fine llama wool blankets. The relationship between humans and dogs had shifted. No longer were dogs living on the periphery of human society. By helping us hunt for food and protect our animals, they were becoming part and parcel of our lives. We were beginning to rely on them.

Chapter 6
Worth Their Weight
In Oxen

Teg at eight months old

To sit with a dog on a hillside on a glorious afternoon is
to be back in Eden.

Milan Kundera, Czech author

If Teg had been born a thousand years ago in Southern Peru into a family of llama herders, I have no doubt that she too would have ended her days buried in woolly finery with a large hunk of llama to sustain her passage to the afterlife. She would at least have had the advantage of working alongside people who knew what they were doing. Stuck with me, poor Teg wasn't being given much of a chance to prove her credentials. Our little flock of ewes and lambs at home rather intimidated her. Because there were so few of them, they were all pretty tame and associated me with a bucket of food or an armful of hay. Every time I opened the gate, the click of the latch would alert them and they'd come running towards me. If there was no food, or I showed any sign of wanting to catch any of them, they would scatter again, and having Teg there made no difference. They weren't remotely wary of her and either ignored her or, if she did dare to approach them, turned to face her head on, stamping their front feet and snorting. In response Teg would retreat swiftly behind my legs or under the gate. 'Some sheepdog!' Ludo said, with not a little sarcasm.

I thought we might have a better chance at the farm with more sheep and bigger fields. I know that sounds a bit counter-intuitive, but Adeline had explained that Welsh dogs, particularly young, inexperienced ones, often work better with larger flocks in lots of space. But it didn't prove to be the magic solution I had hoped for. For a start, as soon as Teg realised that she was going to get a chance to work with sheep her entire personality would change. She would switch from gentle, obedient goofball to unstoppable, uncontrollable delinquent. It didn't matter if she had done a ten-kilometre run with me an hour before; she behaved as if she had been cooped up in a small box for a week and had been given the chance to escape. Instead of heading around the sheep, as she had done so beautifully with Smasher as her mentor, she hurtled like a ginger-and-white missile right through the middle of them, oblivious of my increasingly fraught 'That'll do's. The sheep did the only thing they could in the circumstances. They scattered, headed for the nearest hedge and bunched themselves up tightly against the hawthorn and the nettles where they remained immoveable. There was nothing that I could do or say that would get them out, nor did I know how to ask Teg to help me, or even what I would need her to do. So she would stand in the field, waiting for instruction that never came and looking bemused and hurt as I howled and swore with frustration.

I felt wretched and clearly Teg did too. She slunk out of the field behind me and when I turned back to close the gate she looked up at me, her lovely, mad eyes searching mine for some kind of reassurance. Research at the Clever Dog Lab has shown that another result of dogs' long and close association with us has enabled them to read our facial expressions and our moods. Teg was all too aware that I was cross and upset, but of course couldn't know that my anger was directed only at myself and not at her. I was such a fool to think that I could ever do this. It had only been a couple of years since I had first had sheep at home and I still had so much to learn about them. Whatever had possessed me to think that I could take on a puppy and learn to work with it? What could I possibly teach her apart from how to do everything wrong? I knelt down on the ground. 'I'm sorry, Teg,' I said, wrapping my arms around her, and, loyal, forgiving creature that she is, she pressed her muzzle against my cheek and poked her nose in my ear. But how long would it be before I either put her off working completely or her behaviour became an unbreakable habit that meant she could never reliably work with sheep again? With increasing regularity I found myself lying awake in the middle of the night, replaying my dismal failures over and over again in my head, until one night I hit on a solution that was so obvious I couldn't understand why I hadn't thought of it before. I would give Teg to Adeline. With Adeline she would have a chance to fulfil her potential, even to shine. She would be beautifully cared for and have none of the confusion of being both pet, expected to walk calmly through a field of sheep without even glancing in their direction, and worker with the task of rounding sheep up. It was the only sensible, fair thing to do, I told myself, as hot silent tears poured down my cheeks, behind my ears and seeped into my pillow.

The next morning I walked across the paddock to let Teg out of her stable. As usual she was sitting behind the door, waiting for me, and as soon as I opened it she came snaking out, all warm and smiley and smelling of straw. She stood up on her hind legs, as she always does, and wrapped her front paws around my waist – our early-morning hug. Then she scampered off across the grass in search of Badger and Bella.

Of all the many things that have made life that much more pleasurable since moving to the countryside, it is our pre-breakfast walks that top the list. There is something – I don't know, Zen-like perhaps – about waking up with the sun and the birds, being the first to leave a trail in the dew, seeing the mist rise or the first green shoots poke through the earth. I have found the simple rhythm of walking very therapeutic; it helps to relax and reorder my mind which seems to go into a tailspin at night. It certainly helped me come to a less dramatic, over-wrought solution for Teg the following day. As she bounded ahead, trying to goad Bella to give chase, I decided I would ask Adeline if Teg could stay with her while I was away on a filming trip. I would be gone for a month, giving Teg a proper chance to try and be a sheepdog. Once I got back, I would ask Adeline's advice on the best future for Teg. Calmer, no longer distraught, I walked on, the sun on my face, the air full of butterflies, which Teg found even more entertaining than chasing Bella.

Adeline agreed to take Teg, and it was with a much lighter heart that I packed my bags and flew to Kabul. I was going to film the first programme in a series about shepherding and how it had evolved and changed in the ten thousand years or so since sheep had first been domesticated. We wanted to begin the series in a place where shepherding was still done in a way that had changed little since the very earliest times. It was my idea to go to Afghanistan. A year or two previously I had been there on holiday. I know it sounds like rather an unlikely holiday destination, but I have a friend who owns a travel company specialising in taking people to more unusual places, and he wanted to try out a trekking route in an area of Afghanistan called the Wakhan Corridor. Would I be willing to be a guinea pig and try it out?

The Wakhan Corridor is a thin strip of land right in the north-east of the country, which sticks out like an odd-shaped limb pointing to China. To the south are the dramatic peaks of the Hindu Kush and the Karakoram which form the border with Pakistan. To the north is the Pamir Mountain range and Tajikistan. It is remote and cut off, not just from the rest of the world, but from the rest of Afghanistan too. The people who live there are the Wakhi, Ismaili Muslims who are, without doubt, some of the most welcoming and hospitable people I have ever come across. The valley sits at three thousand metres above sea level, surrounded by towering peaks. A river, fed by lofty glaciers, races through the middle, carving its way through the rocks. Although high and cold, this area has little enough rainfall to be classified as a desert. Winters are long and harsh, the season to grow enough food to sustain both people and their livestock barely four months. Villages are dotted along the length of the valley, connected, but only at certain times of year when the weather allows, by a very rough track, which takes its toll on both vehicles and passengers, and peters out after a couple of hundred kilometres. Anyone travelling further up the valley has to walk, or ride a horse or a yak. Few places have electricity or running water. The houses are built from mud and the stones they have cleared to create tiny, irregular-shaped fields along the banks of the river. An ingenious network of irrigation channels diverts the glacier melt from the mountains to water the fields. The valley has one town, Ishkashim, near the Tajik border. Its few shops – market stalls really – sell cloth to make clothes, hardware like axe heads and scythes, rope, bridles, blocks of salt, sacks of rice and bags of tea. Beyond Ishkashim there are no shops and the Wakhi have to rely on their skills as farmers and the benevolence of Mother Nature to stave off starvation. It is easy, as a westerner, to be charmed by the simplicity of it all; a life free of the tyranny of phones, email and social media; clean air, no light pollution, no constant hum of traffic; home-grown food and free-range children. I was utterly enchanted by the place. I still am, I just know now that life there is far from the idyll it appears. It is a tough, unforgiving existence, borne out by the fact that life expectancy in the Wakhan Corridor is thirty-five years, and more than half the children born die before they are five.

The way the Wakhi live and work with their sheep is probably the closest example of ancient shepherding methods we would find anywhere else in the world. As sheep were almost certainly first domesticated in the Fertile Crescent, geographically the Wakhan Corridor was pretty authentic too. I was heading back, this time with a small film crew, to spend a month living alongside these wonderful people.

The Wakhi diet is pretty basic. They live principally on flat bread, the flour made from the wheat they grow, and tea with milk from either their sheep, goats or yaks. Rice and meat are both luxuries; vegetables, apart from potatoes and wild onions, pretty much unheard of. Because the pressure to grow food is so great, intensified by short summers and lack of space, families drive their sheep and yaks out of the valley and up on to the high mountain pastures so the land they usually graze can be cultivated. Half the family will go with the sheep and camp in yurts for the summer, and the other half stay in the valley to plant and harvest crops. The donkeys and the diminutive local cattle stay as well, as they are used to pull ploughs and thresh wheat when the harvest is brought in. To find the shepherds we had a two-day climb, reaching an altitude of over four thousand metres. When we scrambled, breathless and puffing, up over the final ridge the most glorious sight met our eyes. Spread out in front of us was a wide brown valley, overlooked by towering, snow-covered peaks. Above us in the great blue arch of sky soared a giant bird – a vulture – and in the distance we could just make out a group of yurts and the sheep appeared as specks on the slope behind them.

We stayed with two different communities during our time there and they allowed me to be part of everything they did, from collecting dung as fuel for the fires, to milking (I'm rubbish) and making butter. We got up early in the morning, the high mountain air bitterly cold, and warmed our hands on the udders of the sheep as we coaxed them to give us milk for the first very welcome brew of the day. Then, often I would head out with one of the men, to find good grazing for the sheep. There are no neatly fenced fields or walled enclosures. The sheep roam wherever they want or are encouraged to go by the shepherd. The grazing looked pretty sparse to me: a tough, wiry assortment of vegetation bearing no resemblance to our lush rain-fed Welsh grass at home. But the sheep appeared to thrive on it. They look rather goat-like, mainly because they have hair rather than wool. But the most notable thing about them is that they have enormous, hugely prominent bottoms, for which they are immensely prized. The fat stored in these magnificent posteriors is eaten with great relish throughout the region and presumably the better nourished the sheep, the bigger its bum. The ones I was walking behind could all have rivalled Kim Kardashian, so I am assuming they were finding something good to eat. A couple of the family dogs came along with us, but it seemed more as company for the shepherd as they didn't herd the sheep or help drive them in any particular direction.

Every family had a number of dogs. They were a mixed-looking bunch of all shapes and sizes. If they weren't out with the sheep they would be lying beside the yurts or hanging about eating sheep poo or being played with by the kids. They were very territorial and we were advised not to go too close to them, but with their owners they were as docile as any domestic dog. One family had a particularly fearsome-looking animal, about the size of a Bull Mastiff, which would snarl if any of us came within twenty metres of it, but would allow the tiny daughter of the family to climb on its back and ride it like a Shetland pony.

I noticed one peculiar trait that all the Wakhi dogs seemed to share. They had no ears. The reason? 'There are many predators here. We have bears, snow leopards and wolves. When a wolf attacks a dog it will grab its ears.

That's why we cut the ears off our dogs. It means a wolf can't get hold of them.'

The Wakhi dogs were doing the job their ancestors had been doing since they first started hanging about in the vicinity of human beings: guarding. The difference between then and now is that once humans understood that dogs had an inherent territorial instinct they turned it to their advantage. Even today there are many shepherding communities, not just the Wakhi, that use dogs to guard their flocks. Over the centuries these have been bred to be distinct, recognisable breeds. The gloriously dreadlocked Hungarian sheepdog known as the Komondor may look rather comic, but they will fearlessly protect the animals in their charge. Bruce Fogle, a vet and much-respected author, told me about a friend of his in British Columbia who imported two Komondor puppies to guard his sheep against coyotes. All his neighbours were losing sheep but, as soon as he got the dogs, he didn't lose any. During World War Two many of the Komondors in Hungary were killed because, according to local stories, the invading soldiers had to kill the dog before they could capture the house or farm it guarded. An even older breed is the Italian livestock guardian, the Maremma. Descriptions of this large white dog are found in the writings of Roman scholar Varro, among others. Still used widely in the Abruzzo region of Italy today, their talents have also been employed further afield to protect a very different sort of animal.

While I was out filming in Australia a couple of years ago one of the people I was working with recounted something he'd read in the newspaper that morning. It concerned a colony of little penguins. The little penguin, as the name suggests, is the world's smallest species of penguin. They live on the southern coasts of New Zealand and Australia and have a pretty miserable time of it because not only do their natural predators – New Zealand fur seals and white-bellied sea eagles – want to eat them, but a whole host of introduced species have developed a taste for them too. Dogs, cats, foxes, stoats have all done their bit to diminish numbers. On Middle Island, near Warrnambool, in South-Western Victoria, one colony was reduced from six hundred penguins in 2001 to less than ten in 2005, by foxes. A local chicken farmer came up with an idea. Allan 'Swampy' Marsh had imported a Maremma dog to protect his chickens from foxes and didn't see why it couldn't do the same for the penguins. After much discussion, the idea to let Oddball the Maremma on to the island was agreed. Supervised by environmental scientist Dave Williams, the trial was a success. So much so that there have been Maremmas on the island during the breeding season ever since. Fox kills have ceased entirely and both colony size and breeding success have shown a steady increase. A film was even made in Oddball's honour.

But the time came when humans worked out that dogs could do more than guard livestock and that their instincts as predators had the potential to be useful in other ways. If you want to move your sheep from one place to another it is an awful lot easier doing it with the help of a well-trained dog. I worked on a sheep station north of Perth in Western Australia. It was a million acres – about the size of Kent – and one morning I was asked to help 'gather a paddock'. This paddock, I discovered, was forty kilometres square and full of impenetrable scrubby bush. My job was to sit in a small plane which flew in straight lines above every metre of the field and try and find the sheep. When I did, I radioed down to five blokes on motorbikes, giving the directions so they could go and flush the sheep out. But once the sheep were cleared from the bush the dogs took over, gathered them up and drove them into the sheds.

Although nowadays there are 'sheepdogs' that have been selectively bred to guard and protect livestock, like the Maremmas, and 'sheepdogs' that specialise in herding livestock, like the Border Collie, there are also dogs that make themselves even more invaluable to their human partners by being able to do both, like the Samoyeds of the Nenets.

The Nenets are a nomadic tribe of reindeer herders that live on the Siberian tundra. One winter I went and stayed with a Nenets family. Kostya, his wife Natasha and their daughter Papanaya lived in a tepee – or *chum* – made of reindeer hide and larch poles. They slept on piles of reindeer skins and travelled on sledges made by Kostya and pulled by reindeer. As well as the 'tamer' reindeer that were trained to pull the sledges, they had a herd of about three hundred that were used for breeding, selling and eating. They had a cat called Marushka that lived in the *chum* and travelled in a special box when they moved to a new site, and lots and lots of dogs. Small, with pricked ears, thick coats and tails that curled over their backs, these Samoyeds were multipurpose. They guarded the reindeer, the *chum* and the sledges. They went on hunting expeditions, and watching them herd the reindeer was a delight. They raced tirelessly through the snow, bouncing and barking, and despite their small stature they were fearless, tough and got the job done. Some families use the dogs to pull sledges and I suspect most of them used them in lieu of hot-water bottles on very cold winter nights. Natasha and Kostya had a puppy whose name translated as 'Little Tail'. At first he was very shy and wary, but the longer I stayed the friendlier and more familiar he became. All the other dogs would sleep outside, but when he thought no one was looking, Little Tail would push his way through the door flap and settle down by the fire. On more than one occasion I would wake up and find him curled up on the bottom of my sleeping bag.

Welsh sheepdogs were also bred to have a dual role and it made them hugely valuable. Although there have been no reported ancient grave sites venerating the dogs, they are honoured not just in art and literature, but enshrined in the ancient laws of Wales. The Welsh king Hywel Dda – or to give him his English name, Hywel the Good – was born sometime around AD 880. At that time Wales was a series of separate principalities ruled by different kings, but under the overall rule of the King of England. Hywel was the son of the King of the principality of Seisllwg and when his father died it seems both he and his younger brother took over its rule. But thanks to a handy marriage, the death of his brother, the banishment of a couple of heirs to the thrones of other principalities and a bit of judicious sucking up to the King of England, Athelstan,

Hywel ended up ruling the whole of Wales apart from a bit in the south.

Hywel was well educated with a knowledge of Welsh, English and Latin. He was also fascinated by law, and his studies of legal systems and a pilgrimage to Rome in 928 gave him a radical idea. He gathered together a council of learned folk from all over his kingdom who were tasked to discuss and set down in writing the laws of court, country and of justice. They were known, not terribly surprisingly, as 'The Laws of Hywel the Good' and they were far less draconian than you might imagine. Women's rights were recognised. Marriage was considered an agreement, not a holy sacrament, so divorce was permitted by common consent. Illegitimate children were given the same rights as legitimate ones. But the most compassionate of all was that there was to be no punishment for theft, as long as the sole purpose of the offence was to stay alive. Instead of punishing the thief, the thief had to give compensation to the victim. This common-sense, even-handed approach proved its worth and long after Hywel Dda's death the laws he and his council set out remained active, until the middle of the sixteenth century and the implementation of the Laws in Wales Acts by Henry VIII.

Various copies of the manuscript are kept at the National Library of Wales. It is a handsome, rather imposing building that sits in a commanding position above the town of Aberystwyth and is home to an extensive archive of documents, books and maps relating to Welsh history. There I met the rather wonderful Dr Maredudd ap Huw. Tall, almost translucently pale, white gloves at the ready, he is the library's expert on medieval manuscripts. With him was Cledwyn Fychan, a sprightly eighty-year-old author and historian who probably knows more about Welsh dogs than anyone. Maredudd unloaded a huge, leather-bound tome from a trolley and laid it reverently on the leather-topped table. This particular copy was in Latin, probably written about two hundred years after the original. Maredudd pointed out the passages that referred to the *'Gelgi'* or *'Bukeylky'*. The literal translation is 'buck hound' but, as Cledwyn explained, these were the herdsmen's dogs.

'They could be any sort of dog as long as they could perform certain duties. There were no enclosed fields in those days, so the animals – cattle, sheep, horses – were penned in at night and in the morning, when the animals were let out to graze, the duty of the *bukeylky* was to go in front of the animals to stop them straying and in the afternoon he came behind them, gently driving them back into the pens. Through the night the dog was expected to go three times around the pen to guard the animals from wolves.'

If the neighbours of the herdsman could verify that the dog did indeed perform those duties, then it was protected by law. Maredudd took up the story. 'It is all about function. An animal increases its worth according to what it is doing. In this passage here it states that a hearth cat is worth two pence, but a cat that hunts mice is worth four pence.' These values were important because they dictated the level of compensation required to be given if an animal was stolen or killed. The most valuable animal at the time was the King's stag hound, 'but here is the passage that relates to the *bukeylky*.' And Maredudd ran his gloved finger under the ancient text, translating as he went. 'The herd-dog that goes before the herd in the morning and follows them home at night is worth the best ox.'

So in other words, if I was living in the Middle Ages and someone nicked Teg, they would have to give me a prize ox in compensation. The law demonstrates just how valuable, and valued, these dogs were, although how useful an ox was – however good – to someone who needed to herd and protect their animals is anyone's guess. 'It certainly wouldn't be much good for me,' I said to myself as I drove back home through the hills. 'If I can't even manage to get a sheepdog with all the right instincts to do what she is supposed to, what the hell would I do with an ox?'

Chapter 7
Pulling Power

Matt Hammersley and his team of huskies

Certainly dog driving is the most terrible work one has to face in this sort of business.

Robert Falcon Scott, English explorer, in a
diary entry from the *Discovery* Expedition

The early pastoralists took advantage of the dog's natural territorial and predatory instincts and they proved so effective that even thousands of years later they haven't been surpassed by anything else. Research at the Wolf Science Center has demonstrated that one of the main differences between dogs and wolves – even those raised in an identical way – is that domestication has made dogs more biddable to humans. Wolves are smarter and will learn more, but only if it suits the wolf. Put a piece of meat on a table and tell a dog 'no' firmly, and it will probably resist. A wolf won't. As biologist Raymond Coppinger puts it, 'Dogs are just smart enough to do a job and just dumb enough to do it.' It is probably this factor more than any other that accounts for the fact that dogs have a greater distribution worldwide than wolves have ever had. The willingness to please that dogs developed towards humans was an unbeatable survival strategy. When they were needed to hunt, they hunted, to guard, they guarded, to herd, they herded, and when humans worked out that dogs had yet another potentially useful talent, dogs allowed them to harness that too.

Dogs have pulling power, by which I don't mean they are useful for finding your new love interest. Although perhaps they are if they are now inspiring internet dating sites like 'youmustlovedogsdating.com' and Tindog – 'the Tinder for Dog Owners'. What I'm talking about is a dog's ability to pull. One of the most common complaints dog trainers have to deal with is dogs pulling their owners' arms out of their sockets when they are on a lead. Even my scrawny little mongrel, Badger, all eleven kilos of him, can, on the rare occasions he's on a lead, pull hard enough to make me walk at an unnaturally fast pace and for it to be a huge relief when he doesn't need to be on a lead any more.

I was astonished – and mildly perturbed – to discover that 'weight pulling' competitions exist for dogs. Imagine those strongman competitions where huge, muscle-bound, over-tanned men strain every sinew to pull a plane along a runway. As an aside (and this is the mad world the internet can lead you into) the current Guinness World Record for heaviest aircraft pulled is held by Kevin Fast. He pulled a CL-177 Globemaster III (no, I don't know what that is either) weighing 188.83 tonnes a distance of 8.8 metres. On the Guinness Book of World Records website it appears he did it wearing a dog collar and a large crucifix. On further investigation (thanks, Google) it turns out when he's not pulling planes, tossing cabers and lifting people with his shoulders (he holds the records for those too), he is preaching to the faithful at his local church in Canada where he is the pastor. Anyway, these strength competitions are not confined to humans. Dogs can compete in them too. American Staffordshire Bull Terriers are pretty good at it. Looking not unlike the canine equivalents of Pastor Kevin, they regularly pull over ninety times their body weight. To what end, beyond their owners being able to brag about it in their local bar and post videos on YouTube, I don't know, but it does show that dogs have an innate ability to pull things.

Nowhere is the use of dogs' pulling power more linked to humans than in the Arctic. Historian William J. Mills writes that sledge dogs probably evolved in the area that is modern-day Mongolia. Around 15,000 years ago the people living there undertook a series of migrations which would take them to Siberia, North America and later to Greenland,

and they took their dogs with them. In common with what we believe about dogs' partnership with humans at the time, their dogs would have been used to guard them and to help them hunt. But the descendants of these migrants, the Thule people of North America – ancestors of the modern Inuit – came up with a new idea. Thule archaeological sites dating back 3,000 years always include the remains of dogs, but archaeologists also found evidence of harnesses and other artefacts that indicate the Thule had started using dogs in a way that no one had previously thought of: pulling sledges. It was such a good idea that it too endures to this day.

I found a paper written by the manager of the Iqaluit Research Centre, part of the Science Institute of the Northwest Territories, Canada. Entitled 'The Dogs of the Inuit: companions in survival', it examines how important dogs were to Inuit culture. It describes, among other things, the dogs' incredible predatory skills which would greatly increase the Inuit's chances of finding food. But it is the description of what the dogs are capable of pulling and the conditions in which they will work that is so mind-blowing, it bears being repeated word for word here.

In 1975, Tatigat, a hunter, returned to Igloolik with his dog team after a month of hunting with his family. His *qamotiq* (sledge) was 1.2 by 6.5 metres in length. Forming the base of his tremendous sledge load were, lashed side by side, 14 frozen caribou carcasses, the hindquarters of each fitted neatly into its respective chest cavity. Piled upon this first layer were more than 30 dried sealskins and a number of wadded tarpaulins. The third layer consisted of caribou hide 'sleeping skins', two wooden boxes with a selection of tools and kitchenware, and two steamer trunks. Two whole seals, as yet unfrozen and obtained en route, graced the top of this impressive pile. In front of this load, a washtub lined with a large caribou hide bag was lashed to the *qamotiq*; in the bag were five three-week-old puppies. Travelling across the flat sea ice, 14 sledge dogs pulled the *qamotiq* a distance of 130km over a period of 17 hours. The nursing female joined her puppies at the rest stops to feed them. Also on the *qamotiq* were Tatigat's wife with a small child in her hooded parka and two children under ten years of age. The temperature was −30 degrees centigrade. It is estimated that each dog was pulling at least 100kg. Following a long distance behind were Tatigat's son and daughter (aged 14 and 15) who sat on a 3m *qamotiq* loaded with a huge collection of caribou antlers to be sold to the Hudson Bay store, weighing 130kgs and pulled by a team of five dogs.

A person who drives a team of dogs is called a 'musher'. It is the French we have to thank for the term. In the sixteenth century it was the French who were to become the first Europeans to establish power in Canada and to encourage their dogs to pull their sledges. They would shout '*Marche*!' which became gloriously bastardised to 'Mush!'

Matt Hammersley is a musher. He wasn't born in Alaska or back-country Canada but in the Forest of Dean in Gloucestershire. The Forest of Dean might be considered the Wild West by some, but it is not famed for its long, snowy winters and vast expanse of empty space. So how did he get into sledge-dog racing?

When he was about eleven years old his dad took him to the local cinema. Those of you old enough will remember that in the days before multiplexes and ruinously expensive popcorn, you would get two films for the price of one. There was the main film, but beforehand, instead of endless trailers and adverts for the local curry house – 'just around the corner from this cinema!' – there was another short film. What Matt saw at this little cinema in Coleford was a twenty-minute film about Alaska – all wide open scenery, log cabins and tales of the gold rush. But then came breathtaking scenes of teams of dogs, hitched to sledges, racing across the frozen landscape. They were competing in the Iditarod, a race across a thousand miles of Alaskan wilderness from Anchorage in the south to Nome on the Bering Sea coast in the west. En route, dog teams and their mushers have to endure sub-zero temperatures, storm-force winds that whip up the snow and reduce visibility to nothing, long hours of darkness, treacherous climbs, mountains, frozen rivers, thick forest. It's making me shiver just writing this. But the young Matt was entranced.

'There was this one scene that is for ever ingrained in my memory. I can virtually draw a picture of it. There's this amazing shot from a helicopter of these dog teams coming down this steep mountain valley, twisting and turning and you've just got the snake of this dog team in front and the lead dogs are forty feet away from the sledge because they were running sixteen and even twenty dogs back then. They look like two freight trains coming down through these snowy mountains of Alaska and I'm like wow! That's what I want to do!'

The Iditarod is still run today and is seen as the ultimate of all the sledge-dog races. The race follows the Iditarod Trail, the old mail and supply route with, as Matt told me over our second cup of coffee, a long and dramatic history. The trail was a thousand miles long and linked the coastal towns of Seward and Knik to the mining camps inland and then on to the remote communities, like Unalakleet and Nome on the west coast. The trail would have begun as a network of different trails established by the native Alaskans, who had been using dogs and sledges for centuries to move goods and people about. The incoming Americans were inspired to do the same. This was gold country and the late nineteenth century was the time of the gold rush. The Iditarod Trail must have been like the M6 on a Friday night with thousands of people using it in the hope that it would be a route, if not paved with gold, that would lead them to it. In 1898 when news got out of 'three lucky Swedes' – Jafet Lindeberg, Erik Lindblom and John Brynteson – finding a big haul of gold on Anvil Creek near the little settlement of Nome, it sparked a new rush. People took to the trail again, swelling the population of the town to somewhere between twenty and thirty thousand people.

In less than thirty years the gold rush was over, but the Iditarod Trail remained the vital link between the remote communities that remained. All but about ten thousand people had left Nome, driven away either by promise of riches elsewhere or, more likely, the dark, brutally cold winters. In January of 1925 those remaining people were in desperate peril. Diphtheria struck. Diphtheria is fatal and highly contagious and the town's only doctor, Curtis Welch, had no antitoxin. Without it he knew the whole population could die. He sent a telegram to the US Public Health Service in Washington.

> An epidemic of diphtheria is almost inevitable here
> STOP I am in urgent need of one million units of
> diphtheria antitoxin STOP Mail is the only form of
> transportation STOP

The nearest supply of antitoxin was in Seattle. The authorities could get it as far as the town of Nenana by train but then it was still over six hundred miles to Nome and the only route was the Iditarod Trail. The journey would normally take between twenty-five and thirty days by dog sledge, and there was no other means of transporting the life-saving parcel. But the temperatures across the interior of Alaska that winter were the lowest for twenty years. It was minus 50 degrees centigrade, and high winds were causing the snow to pile up into huge drifts. Dr Welch feared that in those sorts of conditions the efficacy of the antitoxin would last only six days. They had to take a chance: three children had already died and there was no time to lose.

A plan was hatched and the best dog mushers in Alaska – the mail couriers – were organised into a relay across the interior. The antitoxin was packed in glass vials that were then wrapped in padded quilts and packed into a lightweight metal container. It arrived at Nenana station at 9pm on 27 January 1925. By five o'clock on the morning of 31 January the precious package had travelled four hundred miles and reached the coast at Unalakleet. It had been carried by six different dog teams in conditions so brutal that all the mushers had suffered frostbite and hypothermia and three dogs had died. It was still another two hundred miles to Nome and the most treacherous part of the journey lay ahead – the shortcut across the infamous Norton Sound. During the winter the sound freezes, but the ice is in constant motion because of the currents and the incessant wind. The surface can range from glassy-smooth and difficult for the dogs to get traction, to rough hills of ice that have been smashed together. Small cracks can suddenly widen enough to plunge an entire dog team into the freezing water. The wind can be so strong it can flip sledges, drive dogs off course and cause a wind chill of lower than minus 70 degrees centigrade. It takes a very brave, very experienced musher with huge faith in his lead dog to attempt it. That man was Leonhard Seppala.

Seppala had emigrated to Alaska during the Nome gold rush and went to work at the mining company established by Nome's founder and his old friend Jafet Lindeberg. He became the company's dog-sledge driver and quickly gained a reputation as an extremely hard worker who treated his dogs exceptionally well. He took part in his first race – the famously challenging All Alaska Sweepstake – in 1914. He lost the trail in a blizzard, he and his dogs came close to perishing, and he withdrew. With that valuable, if punishing, experience behind him, he spent the intervening year getting himself and his dogs in top racing condition. He was determined to win the race the following year, and he did, beating his far more experienced rival by two hours.

Leonhard Seppala sitting with his dogs

Seppala with his team of dogs, led by Togo, had set off from Nome on 28 January to meet the team that was carrying the antitoxin north up the coast. He crossed the Norton Sound without incident but hit a violent storm on the other side. Knowing that the situation back in Nome was getting increasingly urgent, instead of waiting out the storm, he took the precious cargo, turned Togo and his team around and headed straight back across the exposed ice of the Norton Sound, the storm raging around them.

Togo unflinchingly led the team through the dark in a straight line across the ice, reaching the other side at 8pm. They had covered eighty-four miles in one day in appalling conditions. They rested at a roadhouse until 2am and then set off again. The storm was even worse. The wind was gusting at sixty-five miles an hour and the temperature was minus 40 degrees. They followed the shoreline and then had to climb 1,500 metres to cross Little McKinley mountain where Seppala passed the antitoxin to the next musher, Charlie Olson. It was 3pm on 1 February. In five days Seppala and his dogs had travelled 350 miles. The brutal journey proved to be the last for Togo. It took so much out of him he could never run again.

Olson was blown off course. It took him four hours to reach the next staging post and the antitoxin was passed on to Gunnar Kaasen. Kaasen and his lead dog Balto departed in visibility so restricted that Kaasen often couldn't see the dogs immediately in front of the sledge. The wind by now was so strong it flipped his sledge, flinging the precious container of antitoxin, which had come so far and through such unimaginably hard conditions, into the snow and burying it. Kaasen took off his mitts and plunged his hands into the snow to try and find it. Frostbitten, but successful, he righted the sledge, repacked the container and got to the next staging post where he was due to hand over the antitoxin at 3 o'clock in the morning of 2 February. Remarkably, he was ahead of schedule and the next musher was still asleep. The weather was finally improving, Balto and the team were still running well, so Kaasen pressed on. He reached Nome a couple of hours later, at 5.30am. The antitoxin had travelled 674 miles in 127 hours and 30 minutes in extreme conditions and, when it was removed from the container and unwrapped from the quilts, not a single vial was broken. It was thawed out and by midday Dr Welch was vaccinating the people of Nome. The epidemic was halted in its tracks.

The mushers and their dogs who had saved Nome were hailed as heroes by press and public alike. They received medals, letters from the President and thousands more from people all around the country. Yet, Matt told me sadly, it wasn't long before planes took over the job of delivering mail, and the Iditarod Trail was no longer the lifeline of Alaska. A further blow came in the 1960s when thousands of years of Arctic history were almost eradicated. Joseph-Armand Bombardier had invented the snowmobile.

'It was like the equivalent of our industrial revolution,' Matt said, pouring more coffee. 'People called them "iron dogs". They could just bung some fuel in them. They didn't have to feed them, they didn't have to train them or exercise them. They didn't have to breed them. It was just a machine. No one wanted sledge dogs any more. Come the Sixties the breeds were dying out, the bloodlines were dying out.'

With the decline of the dogs came the decline of the sport of sledge-dog racing. The first documented sledge-dog race was in 1850. It started in Winnipeg, Manitoba and ended over five hundred miles away in St Paul, Minnesota. It was probably an informal affair but by the turn of the century the sport was gaining in popularity. Nome became the sort of sledge-dog racing equivalent of Ascot, spurred on, Matt surmised, by all those miners wanting to have something to bet on. Throughout the 1920s and 1930s the sport continued to grow and prosper throughout North America. Once snowmobiles took over from dogs, it seemed the sport was destined to die out.

'It was saved,' Matt told me, reverently, 'by a man called Joe Redington.'

Joe Redington moved up to Knik River in Alaska, on the route of the old Iditarod Trail, in 1948. By then the trail had pretty much been swallowed up by the wilderness. He established a kennel to breed sledge dogs and he, and later his wife, set about clearing part of the old trail and worked as hunting guides. It was not a good time to be a musher. Before Joe's very eyes dog sledging was becoming a thing of the past. He wrote, 'When I visited interior villages in the 1950s, every household had five or six dogs. They were the only transportation. But by the late 1960s village dogs were almost gone.'

But a meeting with Dorothy Page was to give dog sledging a renewed lease of life. Dorothy was the president of the committee in charge of organising events to celebrate the hundredth anniversary of the purchase of Alaska from Russia. A self-confessed 'history buff', she wanted 'a spectacular dog race to wake Alaskans up to what mushers and their dogs had done for Alaska'. The problem was, none of the few remaining mushers were interested in supporting the idea, until she met Joe. Joe, who had been fighting to get the Iditarod Trail recognised as a National Historic Trail since the Fifties, agreed, but stipulated that the race needed to be along part of the old trail and the prize money needed to be spectacular. In February 1967, fifty-eight mushers competed along a twenty-five-mile stretch of the Iditarod Trail for the chance to win $25,000. Joe hoped the race would become an annual event, but the following year it was cancelled because – bizarrely – there wasn't enough snow, and in 1969 only $1,000 was raised as prize money, and only twelve people took part. But Joe was not prepared to give up. Instead he decided to make the race more challenging and the prize money even greater. The route would run to Nome – a thousand miles away – and the prize money raised came to $51,000. Dorothy Page helped form the organising committee and the race took place in 1973. It marked a revival in dog sledging, which has grown exponentially ever since. The Iditarod has become world-famous, and Alaska now hosts a huge number of major races every winter.

The footage of the Iditarod that so captured Matt's imagination when he was a child and the impression it left never lessened. He would go for walks with his parents on Sundays in the forest, look at the tracks and dream of running a dog team down them. Every Christmas and every birthday he'd ask for a husky puppy even though he had never seen one and wasn't even sure if they existed in the UK. It was at a dog show that he realised that at least part of his dream was in reach. His parents were there showing their terrier and he was hanging around, 'bored stupid'. So he wandered into another hall and there he saw Siberian Huskies being shown. 'And I thought – I know what these dogs are! I recognise them! They do exist here!

– and I spent the whole of the rest of the day watching them.' What Matt didn't know then was that huskies first came to Britain in 1968 and small races were being held, using wheeled chariots rather than sledges.

By the time Matt got to university his dream of being a musher hadn't diminished. His friends Ian and Nicky had two Siberian Huskies and trained them for racing. Matt helped out, learning everything he could, and finally in 2002, he was able to fulfil the dream he'd had since he was a child: to get a Siberian Husky of his own and race. He named his puppy Kirra and, thinking of my own experience with Teg, I was intrigued how he started training her when he'd never done it before. He told me that all the time he had spent with Ian and Nicky and their dogs really helped. He'd learned that the first thing he had to do was teach Kirra the commands. Contrary to popular belief, mushers don't actually use 'Mush!' as a command any more. The main ones the dogs need to learn are 'Gee' (turn right) and 'Haw' (turn left). Every time Matt took Kirra for a walk he would use those commands and reward her when she got it right. But he couldn't use treats or any kind of food as reward, it all had to be in his voice. 'Because we can't stop if they take a correct turn on the trail and give them more Bonios, because then we've lost the race!'

Once Kirra was old enough and more confident, Matt started to run her with Ian and Nicky's lead dog Buffy and it was from Buffy that Kirra really started to learn how to hone her pulling instincts. Their first race was in Grimsthorpe, a sprint over 3.8 miles. Ian and Nicky lent Buffy to Matt to race alongside Kirra. 'I was nervous as hell,' Matt laughed. 'I got my race number, I looked at my start time, got my race kit on, got to the start line and both the dogs sat down. They're not bouncing up and down like normal. I start thinking, are they even going to run?'

The countdown started and still the dogs didn't move. Matt's heart was racing. 'Ten, nine, eight, seven, six, five . . . and then the dogs were up in the air, bouncing and barking and as soon as they were released they were off. And at that second all my nerves vanished. It was just me and my dogs and the training takes over. I got round and it was amazing, absolutely amazing. I couldn't wait to do it again. I was hooked.'

He asked me if I'd ever been on a dog sledge?

'I have, once,' I told him, 'on a brief filming trip in Greenland.'

We had flown from Iceland the short distance across the Greenland Sea to a small settlement in the south-east corner of the country. In the summer this area is a collection of small islands but this was early March and the narrow stretches of water between the islands were frozen. It was impossible to see where the land ended and the sea began. We unloaded our bags and equipment from the plane, piled them on to sledges and were taken by snowmobile to town. Neat, functional buildings dotted the slopes, snow lay in thick layers on all the roofs and piled in drifts deep enough to disappear in. The only shop sold no fresh goods at all, but cans of spaghetti, fishing equipment and chunks of seal in vacuum packs. We ate some seal. I can't say I'd relish the chance to try it again. As we walked through this most alien of landscapes we realised that the small grey mounds outside many of the houses were in fact dogs, curled up tight, their tails over their faces.

We were filming with traditional hunters and the next morning we went to meet them. We arrived, bundled up in layers of merino wool and goose down, to find the three men preparing their sledges. There seemed to be dogs everywhere, howling and yipping and straining at their tethers. We were warned not to touch them as they were unused to strangers and they paid little heed to us. Harnesses were passed over their heads and they were attached in pairs either side of a long line that ran from the front of the sledge. One man indicated where I should sit and, with me perched on a pile of skins, together with various fearsome-looking tools and coils of rope, we set off, the hunter running for a few metres alongside the sledge before jumping on. The dogs' behaviour changed instantly. They switched from being an unruly, seemingly wild, pack to a harmonious team the moment they were given the command to set off.

We were travelling to the edge of the sea ice in search of seals. The journey would take about two hours and gave us a chance to fully appreciate the quite magnificent landscape we were in. I think I had expected it to be a featureless, monochrome expanse of flat ice, but it was anything but. Icebergs, trapped at the start of the winter, rose up like immense sculptures of blue and translucent glass. The low sun gave out no heat but lit up the snow and ice in every shade of orange and pink. The silence was almost tangible, broken only by the swish of the sledge's runners, the soft, rhythmic padding of the dogs' paws and the jarring shouts of the director who – unlike me – hadn't forgotten that we were actually here to film stuff.

But several hours into the journey – filming can be a very slow process, particularly in temperatures cold enough to freeze lenses and tripods – I have to admit the novelty of the experience was beginning to wear off. I am not very good at being inactive at the best of times. I drive my husband mad because I can barely sit still long enough to watch a film. But being inactive on a sledge at a very chilly time of year leads to one screamingly obvious inevitability. You get cold. Despite my high-tech layering, Arctic mitts and specialist boots I began to get so cold I couldn't think straight, or speak in any sort of coherent way, which, given my job, was unfortunate. And another thing that you don't read about on all the glossy dog-sledging websites is that the dogs – well, these dogs anyway, fed as they are on great hunks of seal – shit copiously and potently on the run; sitting downwind of them you are all too aware of the fact.

Matt laughed. 'It'll be a bit different here. How good are you at getting up early?'

'Very good!' I answered truthfully. 'I just struggle to stay awake beyond 10pm.'

'Great, then meet me here tomorrow morning at six . . . no, better make it five thirty. It's not forecast to be a hot day, but it'll give us a bit more time before it gets too warm for them to run. Wear clothes that you don't mind getting dirty. They will be covered in mud and paw prints by the time we're done.'

'All my clothes are permanently covered in mud and paw prints. I'll see you tomorrow.'

I arrived, bang on time, to see a large van parked outside Matt's shop, covered in logos and 'Tanglefoot', the name of Matt's team, emblazoned on the side. As I walked over to say good morning a chorus of barks started up from inside the van. 'Come and meet them,' said Matt, and slid open the door. Inside was fitted out with a wall of cages and from each one peered a bright-eyed, eager little face. 'They are all pure bred Siberian Huskies,' said Matt. 'Different ages and different levels of experience. Some are siblings or the offspring of others.'

'How many have you got now?'

'Eleven, but Wolfe here' – and he ruffled the head of a rather large, stately-looking dog who was sitting on a bed in the back rather than in a cage – 'he's retired and up there is Kirra, my original dog. She's retired too, but I think she would still run given the chance. I always bring them with me because they hate being left behind.'

'And where do you keep them all?' I asked. 'Do they live in kennels?'

'They've got the downstairs run of the house and the garden. Wolfe, here, who's like a big old bear, spends probably twenty-three hours of the day outside. He's an outdoor dog. He's got a kennel in the garden and he sleeps out there at night, but we leave the kitchen door open so he can come in and out if he wants to. The rest, to be honest, are right softies. They're these big tough dogs that are supposed to be living in minus fifty in the wilds of the Arctic and Alaska and Siberia, eating seals, but no, they want to cuddle up on the sofa, they want to lie in front of the log burner. Invariably, my wife gets the pick of the sofa with the dogs and I get what's left, perched on an arm or something!'

I wondered what sort of bond he had – could possibly have – with so many dogs. 'The bond we have is incredibly strong. When we're working these dogs we've got to put our complete trust in them and they've got to have complete trust in us, otherwise it doesn't work.'

I told him I believe Teg truly comes into her own when she's working, that although she was perfectly content chasing a Frisbee around with the other dogs or lying draped on a sofa, she would be even happier on a mountain with no fences and hundreds of sheep to gather up. Matt nodded. 'These dogs are the same. They absolutely love to work. They haven't run since May, when it started to get too warm. We don't train them in the summer, but they knew exactly where we were driving to this morning. As soon as I got my boots out of the cupboard at home they went mental.'

Matt hitched up a trailer to his van, drove a quad bike on to it and set off. After a couple of miles he turned off on to a forestry track and pulled in at a clearing. I stood and watched a routine that was clearly much practised. Matt opened the back of the van to reveal all manner of bits of kit, neatly stacked, coiled and slung. He asked me to knock two heavy stakes into the ground, a line was rigged up between them with short tethers leading off that at equal distances. Then the dogs were taken out of the van, leaping with pent-up energy and excitement and attached to the line.

'This gives them a chance to stretch, to have a poo — there's a bucket and a shovel there if you wouldn't mind scooping it up — and this is where they start to get psyched up. They know they are about to run. We do this every time they go out and before every race.'

It was my first chance to get a really good look at the dogs. The Siberian Husky is an undeniably good-looking animal. With their luxuriant grey coats, short pricked ears and athletic build, they manage to look both wolf-like and cuddly at the same time. A myth persists that huskies are indeed more closely related to wolves than other breeds of dog, but that is simply not true. Studies prove they are no more closely related to wolves than Chihuahuas. What is true, is that like Teg, they have a hardwired instinct to work, not to herd sheep, but to run and pull. Their looks have made them one of the most popular of the Nordic breeds to keep as a pet, but, as Bruce Fogle writes, 'Siberian Huskies are great at finding open gates, gaps in fences, other dogs to challenge, flower beds to dig and cats to chase. If you are looking for a house dog, look elsewhere.'

Matt agrees. 'These dogs have been carefully bred for thousands of years to pull sledges. That desire to work — their absolute passion for sledge-dog work — is immense. But they are a joy to work with because they are such characters. My dogs are a complete mix. Some are quiet, some are thinkers — super intelligent, and they often end up being lead dogs. Some are very loving and are all cuddly and cute. Zoya is a clown with the best sense of humour I have ever seen in a dog.'

Matt brought out the harnesses from the back of the

van, sending the dogs into a renewed frenzy of excitement. He showed me how to put them on – they weren't complicated but the dogs were so excited it took a while to ensure that all the right limbs were through the right holes. Then Matt led them one by one to a line attached to the quad bike and positioned them according to their strengths and experience.

'What are they going to pull?' I asked. There was no sign of any sort of cart or wheeled sledge.

'The quad bike,' said Matt. 'Jump on!'

I was incredulous. I know sledge dogs are famed for their strength and stamina, but sledges are designed to run as efficiently on snow as they can. It was late August in the Forest of Dean. There was no snow. Could eight dogs really pull a quad bike with Matt and me on board along a grassy track? He started the engine. 'We give them a little bit of throttle, just to get going, and a bit more just to help with the hills. It is their first day training since May so we'll take it a bit easy with them.'

Matt released the brakes and we were off, the dogs streaking out in front of us in perfect formation. A quad bike being pulled through the Forest of Dean perhaps doesn't sound the most romantic of images and it was rather noisier than a sledge, but it was also warmer and a lot less smelly than my previous experience. The dogs ran a mile circuit and to my inexperienced eyes it appeared they had been working beautifully, especially given they hadn't worked for a while. Matt was pleased too, and confident enough that once they had had a breather, to offer me a go.

I climbed on the quad bike and looked at the line of dogs in front of me. There are no reins, nothing that physically connected me to the dogs. All I had to do was give them the verbal instructions and steer the quad bike. Matt sat behind me.

'Ready?' he asked. I nodded. He released the brake and the dogs streaked away. Of course they didn't run as well for me as they did for Matt. Kapik, one of the lead dogs, really tested me, almost stopping at one point and throwing the rest of the team into a state of brief disarray, but with the help of Matt I got them going again and came down the final hill and along the home stretch feeling madly exhilarated. At that moment I started to understand why dog sledging has so entranced Matt for almost his entire life, how Leonhard Seppala and the other incredible dog-sledge mushers who saved the population of Nome did what they did. Somehow when you have a team of dogs running in front of you, you feel invincible.

Chapter 8
To The Ends Of The Earth

Tim Fogg in Antarctica

I've seen a look in dogs' eyes, a quickly vanishing look of amazed contempt, and I am convinced that basically dogs think humans are nuts.

John Steinbeck, American author, in *Travels with Charley*

Of course, not all of us have eleven Siberian Huskies to help us feel invincible, but an early-morning walk or run with my smaller, less pedigree pack does make a good start to a day. There are never any grumblings or moanings about being dragged out of bed – instead I am greeted with much ecstatic wagging and smiling, and as soon as I open the door, whatever the weather, they bounce outside with an enthusiasm which is infectious. Each day is an adventure full of new smells and the beguiling possibility of squirrels racing across the track or pheasants lurking in a hedge. To run with dogs through fields and woods in the early morning, the first rays of the sun stealing up over the hill, with birds providing the soundtrack, is pretty much unbeatable. Badger and Teg bound ahead, leaping stiles, oblivious of hills, while Bella and I are the two middle-aged ladies at the back, shuffling contentedly along at our own pace and admiring the scenery. Returning home, a bit sweaty and red-faced, but stocked up on fresh air and endorphins, stands me in pretty good stead for most days. However, I have found myself in a few situations when it would be very nice to be able to feel invincible; when I've had to dig deep into my reserves of courage which lurk quite a bit below my much more accessible reserves of fear. Luckily, though, I know a man called Tim Fogg who is definitely my equivalent of eleven huskies. Possibly more.

I first met Tim, climber, caver and rope access specialist, when I did a television project exploring underground Britain. I had been into a few caves before, but only the great cavernous ones that are reached by well-trodden, well-lit routes, where you might be advised to wear sensible shoes and a warm coat and be issued with a helmet only to satisfy some slightly over-cautious health and safety concern. I had never been into the sort of cave that required me to wear a wetsuit, Gore-Tex overalls and a climbing harness. I had never had to wade in the pitch dark through freezing water up to my chest, slither and slide my way down chutes that dropped into a dark unknown, inch my way along vertiginous ledges and wriggle through tunnels so tight even a Jack Russell would have found it claustrophobic. I did this, on and off, for several weeks. I was scared every day; there were some days when I was almost paralysed with terror, but I managed not only to complete the project but also, in a weird sort of way, to really enjoy it, and that was, in no small way, down to Tim. He has a sort of magical ability to make you believe that you are capable of things that, were he not there, you wouldn't dream of attempting. He has a bottomless well of patience, is utterly calm and unflappable, is as persuasive as he is encouraging and in the end you feel compelled to do whatever it is he is trying so hard to help you to do because letting him down is unthinkable.

Tim made me believe that I could climb Castleton Tower in Utah. I am not a climber and have a healthy fear of falling off things, and if you look at pictures of Castleton Tower you will see that falling off it looks much easier than climbing it. We travelled to Moab, Utah's adventure hub, did some training and waited for the weather forecasters to tell us when would be a good day to make our ascent. A couple of blustery, wet days kept us grounded and to kill time I would wander down Moab's only street and spend a happy hour or so in the local bookshop. Except that on the second day, when my nerves were getting the better of me, I did a very silly thing. I picked up a book that was a guide to some of the climbing routes in the area. I flicked to the section on Castleton Tower. There were pictures of tiny figures clinging God-only-knows-how to a sheer, vertical rock face. I started to cry with fear. Yet at 4.30 the next morning I was driving to the point where you hike in to the start of the climb and ten hours later I was standing on the top of Castleton Tower, tear-stained, adrenalin-fuelled and elated, looking out at the magnificent world beneath my feet.

'Told you you could do it!' said Tim.

So when an executive producer at the BBC asked if I would be prepared to abseil into the crater of a permanently erupting volcano on a distant South Pacific Island for a science programme I didn't hesitate. 'I'll do it as long as Tim Fogg is there.'

Vanuatu is a chain of islands that sits on what is known as the Pacific Ring of Fire. All the islands are there thanks to seismic events and the archipelago still has nine active volcanoes. I was to collect rock and gas samples from inside the crater of Marum on the island of Ambrym. Marum has a permanent lava lake, an immense super-heated cauldron of molten rock that is constantly bubbling and spitting and lights up the night sky with an eerie orange glow. I would be dangling on a rope right above it.

Once again we needed the right weather, and conditions on the top of Marum are famously volatile. Storms can blow in from nowhere, the cloud can descend until it is impossible to see, wind can whip up the dust, fill the air with toxic gases and turn rain into a horizontal, blinding deluge. It was on a morning like this that we sat, huddled under a flapping tarpaulin, nursing plastic mugs of tea. Tim asked what else I was up to and I told him I was in the midst of researching a book that looked at the extraordinary and enduring relationship between humans and dogs.

'There is nothing like it, that bond you get with a dog,' said Tim. 'I used to work with dog teams in Antarctica.'

'What?!' I cried, thinking, is there nothing this man can't do? 'When were you in Antarctica?'

'The late Seventies,' he said. 'Looks like the weather's clearing. We might have a window, but we can't muck about. I don't want either of us on the ropes if another storm comes in like that. Ready? Don't forget your gas mask!'

Tim's father, Gordon Elliott Fogg, went to school at Dulwich College, the same school as the famous polar explorer Ernest Shackleton. Shackleton's boat from his Trans-Antarctic Expedition of 1914–16, the *James Caird*, was presented to the school after Shackleton's death in 1922. Tim told me his father used to avoid games, which he hated, and would sit with Shackleton's boat and dream of his own trip to Antarctica. Gordon Fogg became a professor of marine biology, and went on to work for many years at the British Antarctic Survey, travelling to the continent three times. There is even an area called Fogg Highland which is named after him. When Tim finished his postgraduate teaching training in 1974 it was his father who suggested he start his working life in the Antarctic. He went for an interview and got a job as a marine assistant working on the island of South Georgia in the Southern

Ocean for two and a half years. He came back to the UK, but after only nine months was once again hankering to return to the Antarctic. This time he was posted to the British Antarctic Survey base Rothera. He was supposed to be there just for the summer, but the base cook had an accident and Tim was asked if he would stay out and take over catering duties. It was during that winter of 1978–79 that he learnt how to drive a team of dogs.

Dogs had been introduced to Antarctica on a permanent basis by the precursor to the British Antarctic Survey, the Falkland Islands Dependencies Survey, in 1944. Their principal purpose was to pull the sledges needed to further the scientific study and exploration of the continent. They remained invaluable in Antarctica longer than anywhere else because no one came up with a machine reliable and robust enough to withstand the extreme climate and challenging terrain. Throughout the Sixties and Seventies, when dog sledging became almost relegated to history in the Arctic, most of the nations with bases in Antarctica were using dogs. The dogs, huskies from Greenland and Arctic Canada, are an ancient breed thought to be directly descended from the dogs brought to Greenland by the first Inuit settlers. They are known for their strength, speed and endurance, but not the easiest of temperaments, as Tim was to discover.

The dogs at Rothera in 1979 had all been born and bred in Antarctica and one of the teams, known as the Huns, was looked after by Nigel Young. By then mechanisation had taken over and the dog teams were used largely for recreational purposes, particularly during the long winters. It was Nigel who took Tim out with the dogs for the first time.

'It was absolutely captivating but complete mayhem. I was run over by the sledge, the dogs got into fights, they were just incredibly hard to manage,' said Tim, with a rueful laugh. The team consisted of nine dogs, attached to a single central trace in pairs with the lead dog at the front. But getting them on to the trace was a challenge in itself. The dogs were chained about two metres apart in what is called a span. That is where they slept, curled up in tight balls, their thick fur well adapted to prevent them getting frostbitten and their tails long enough to wrap around their noses. It was also where they were fed. To prepare them for the sledge they needed to be taken off the span, have their running harness put on and then be attached to the trace which was held firm by steel pickets knocked into the snow. And, Tim said, these dogs are absolutely mad keen, howling and barking and pulling to run. Matt Hammersley's dogs were the same. As soon as they know that they are going to get a run in front of a sledge it is all you can do to hold them. Tim told me that sometimes the dogs were so keen they would pull at the trace so hard that the ice pickets would be dragged out and then they would be off without you. It happened to him more than once – 'All you can do is hope to grab hold of the length of rope that is tied on to the back of the sledge.'

At the end of the rope is what Tim called 'a monkey's fist' – a large knot that prevents your hands slipping right off the end of the rope while you are being dragged behind, 'and it is either your howling that makes them stop, or something else, like they start fighting. It was wonderful chaos!'

But Tim's diary records that over that winter he got more practised and the dogs would sometimes – but not always – do what he wanted them to do. 'I went out one day and there was about an hour when the dogs behaved brilliantly. It was just stunning; on my own, with these nine dogs running over snow and ice and they actually responded to my commands, even stopped when I wanted them to.' I asked him how it compared to being on a Skidoo.

'It just feels far more adventurous and far more intense. The dogs are of paramount importance to your survival. There were no aircraft over winter in Antarctica in those days. If you were a hundred and twenty miles from base and a dog got injured or fell down a crevasse or didn't do what you wanted it to do and got you stuck, you were stuffed. You had to build a bond with them. It was teamwork and every time we stopped, which we would do every hour for fifteen minutes or so, I would make my way down the line of dogs, cuddling them, praising them, particularly the lead dog. They liked affection but they also had to know you were in charge otherwise you didn't stand a chance.'

Tim clocked up about six hundred miles with the dogs that winter, sledging across the sea ice and up on to the spine of the Antarctic peninsula. On his best days he would cover thirty miles in nine hours, pulling a sledge carrying eight hundred kilos of equipment and supplies for him and the dogs. On his worst day he covered just over half a mile in nine hours.

'Why?' I gasped.

'We were on soft snow and slush. The sledge probably tipped over twenty times and every time it does that you have to unload eight hundred kilos of stuff, right it and reload it. On a bad day it was just awful.'

It was an awful day with dogs that almost certainly put paid to Robert Falcon Scott's ambition to be the first to reach the South Pole. The existence of the Antarctic continent was unknown until January 1820 when it was first sighted by a Russian expedition. A year later two American sealers were the very first humans to set foot on the Antarctic land mass, going ashore at Hughes Bay to look for seals. Their achievement was overlooked and it was a Norwegian whaling expedition much later, in 1895, that lay claim to putting the first people on shore. One of them was a Norwegian-born, half-British schoolmaster called Carsten Borchgrevink and he returned as the leader of the British Antarctic Expedition in 1898. He brought with him two Sami dog-handlers from northern Norway and seventy-five dogs – the first to reach Antarctica. Dogs' long association with man had meant that they had now reached all seven continents of the world.

Borchgrevink's expedition was the first of many attempts to further explore this completely uncharted territory. In 1901 a Swedish expedition also took dogs and sledges and with them covered 380 miles of a previously unknown part of the coast in thirty-three days, but their exploration was forced to come to a hasty end when, during a storm, the dogs discovered a sack containing the men's food supplies and ate the lot, including part of the sack. Hot on the heels of this expedition came one that was led by Robert Falcon Scott. There were fifty members of the expedition team, including one Ernest Shackleton, but not one of them had any Antarctic or even Arctic experience. They took dogs and skis with them, but Scott became convinced that neither were of any benefit to travelling across the ice, instead advocating the man-hauling of sledges as the only way to travel. The dogs almost certainly didn't perform well, but probably because no one knew how to look after and feed them properly or how to handle them. The experience left a bad impression on Shackleton and when he later made his own attempt to reach the South Pole he took ponies and a specially adapted motorised vehicle. The car proved unable to drive on anything other than flat ice and none of the ponies survived. Although they got further south than anyone had done before, they failed to reach the pole.

When Scott set out on the *Terra Nova* in 1910 with the express aim of beating Shackleton and reaching the pole, he took dogs as well as ponies and motorised sledges. The dogs had been bought in Siberia by expedition member Cecil Meares. The expedition photographer, Herbert Ponting, described them in his book *The Great White South*. They were, he wrote, 'strange beasts':

> They harked back to a wild ancestry – wolves. Some of
> them even now were more like wolves than dogs; others
> seemed nearer akin to coyotes – with their sharp snouts
> and foxy-looking eyes. Only in their massive forelegs did
> they resemble the heavier North American 'husky'; but

they made no bones about undertaking a husky's work. Though the biggest of them turned the scale at under 80lbs, a team of eleven would sometimes pull a load of a 1,000lbs to Hut Point, fifteen miles away, in four hours; while with lighter loads they would make the journey in ninety minutes. They were always ready for work; indeed they seemed to regard work as the only sort of fun to be had in these regions – and they were not far wrong.

But then came the awful day when Scott, along with two other members of the team, Apsley Cherry-Garrard and Edward Wilson, set off with Meares, ten dogs and a sledge. The dogs fell down a crevasse, and the men just managed to anchor the sledge in time to stop it going down too. Eight of the dogs could be hauled out by their harnesses but Scott had to be lowered down into the crevasse to rescue the other two. It was a very lucky escape, but, as Tim told me, that was one of the great advantages of travelling with dogs. 'If you are on a Skidoo and it breaks through a snow bridge and falls down a crevasse, you go with it. Horrible as it sounds, if the dogs go first, you have a chance to save yourself and you can often pull the dogs out because the harnesses will stop them falling out of reach.' But Scott didn't see it that way. He wrote, 'Bit by bit I am losing all faith in the dogs.'

Scott's planned route to the South Pole was to set off from Cape Evans and head for the pole via the Beardmore Glacier – a return journey of 1,700 miles. He would use a combination of the motorised sledges – which hadn't proved a great success and only two were still working –

the ponies and the dogs to get them and supplies to the base of the glacier. At that point the ponies would be shot for food, the dogs would return to base and the men would haul the sledges the rest of the way.

Scott was aware that there was a rival expedition led by Norwegian explorer Roald Amundsen, who believed that skis and sledge dogs were the most efficient way of travelling in the polar regions. To this end his team included a skilled ski-maker and the best dog-sledge drivers he could find, as well as an excellent cook. He couldn't understand the British aversion to dogs: 'Can it be that the dog has not understood its master? Or is it the master who has not understood the dog?' Amundsen travelled to the Antarctic with one hundred Greenland Huskies and, while Scott used ponies to set up his supply depots, Amundsen used the dogs and learnt valuable lessons by doing so. He discovered the optimum weight dogs could pull without struggling and getting too exhausted, and decided to increase the number of dogs he would take with him on his attempt to reach the South Pole.

He set off on 8 September 1911 – a risk, as it was still winter and although temperatures had risen to a positively balmy minus 27 degrees centigrade, it wasn't to last. A few days later the temperature was once again below minus 50 and the dogs' paws were getting frostbitten. Knowing that both dogs and men were now in danger, Amundsen turned the party back, but en route was hit by a strong headwind; several dogs froze to death. He waited another month, until 19 October, before he set out again with four other men, four sledges and fifty-two dogs.

The motorised vehicles of Scott's expedition set off on 24 October 1911 but broke down after only fifty miles, and the four drivers had to man-haul all the supplies 150 miles. Scott left on 1 November with the ponies and dogs and they all met near the foot of the Beardmore Glacier on the 21st as planned. The ponies were shot for food and the dogs were returned to base. The men continued their journey south man-hauling the sledges.

Amundsen was making good progress. He was taking a different route, one that no one had done before. He was full of praise for the dogs. Seven had perished but forty-five remained. However, some of them were going to be sacrificed to supply the men with meat. 'There was depression and sadness in the air; we had grown so fond of our dogs.' Eighteen dogs were left to accompany the party to the pole, which they reached on 14 December 1911. By the time they returned to their base they had travelled almost 2,200 miles in ninety-nine days. Eleven of the fifty-two dogs had survived and were given to the Australasian Antarctic Expedition led by Douglas Mawson.

Scott and his party reached the South Pole over a month later on 17 January 1912. None of them survived the return journey.

Amundsen's success was helped exponentially by his use of skis and dogs and his experience of icy conditions. Perhaps it was his journey that inspired the introduction of dogs to the British Antarctic research bases in 1944 and the Australian ones a decade later. The British and Australians continued to use dogs in Antarctica far longer than any of the other nations, but in 1991 an Antarctic

Treaty stated that as non-indigenous species, 'dogs shall not be introduced on to land or ice shelves and dogs currently in those areas shall be removed by April 1st 1994'.

When travel writer Sara Wheeler was writer-in-residence in Antarctica she came across a telex from the Foreign Office in the archives at the Rothera research station. It suggested the breeding of dogs should cease, since mechanical transport was taking over. It was dated 1963, fifteen years before Tim Fogg arrived at Rothera and long before the treaty. It was scrawled over by indignant comments and ignored. But the 1991 treaty had to be adhered to. In 1993 the last dogs left the Australian Mawson base and in the winter of 1993 two men, John Killingbeck and John Sweeny, set out from Rothera with the two remaining dog teams, the Huns and the Admirals. Killingbeck wrote, 'Our journey was a final farewell to these dogs and a "thank you" to generations of loyal, friendly animals . . . The bond between working animal and man is a very special one. In Antarctica their life depends on you and your life on them.'

Tim echoed that sentiment. 'It was absolutely pure adventure, an extraordinary experience. There has been no other time in my life when I have had a bond with an animal like that. It was fantastic.'

Chapter 9
Lost And Found

Missy and her puppies

Dogs do speak, but only to those who know how to
listen.

Orhan Pamuk, Turkish author, in *My Name is Red*

Once home from Afghanistan, it was with mixed emotions
that I drove north, through Hereford and out the other
side towards Adeline's farm. Much as I had loved being
with the Wakhi I had, by the end of my month away,
started to feel a little homesick. I was never homesick
before we moved to Wales, but perhaps that's because I

never really felt at home in London. And we didn't have dogs then. There have been multiple surveys done that reveal that the majority of pet owners miss their pets more than their family when they go away and I suspect – OK, I know – I'm part of that majority. But excited as I was at the thought of seeing Teg, I hadn't forgotten the resolution I'd made before I left. I would only keep Teg if it was best for her. If she was going to be better off with Adeline, or if Adeline recommended she go to someone else, I would let her go. I hastily brushed away the tears that spilled over the minute I contemplated life without my adored ginger-and-white dog and turned into the lane that runs up to Adeline's house.

'Go and get her,' said Adeline after we had done our hellos. 'She's in the trailer. We'll show you what we've been up to.' Teg looked really well, sleek and fit. And although she had clearly thrived in Adeline's care, I was both relieved and happy that she seemed as excited to see me as I was to see her. She leapt out of the trailer, ran off, ran back, jumped up and flung her paws around my waist, ran off and back again, skidded to a halt at my feet and gazed up at me adoringly.

'Come on, daft dog,' I said and she galloped ahead, anticipating, perhaps, a chance to show off and be admired, which is what she loves best.

We walked with Adeline back down the lane and clambered over a gate into a bordering field. The first thing I noticed was that Teg was walking to heel. If she strayed too far ahead, Adeline told me to slap my coat or leg, and the effect was instantaneous. As soon as she heard the noise, Teg would pause, wait for me to catch up and then walk on, her head level with my knee. When we got to the gate she jumped clean over it. From very early on, her brother Taff could leap hurdles, stiles and fences with ease and grace, although not always at opportune moments. Teg, on the other hand, had always been a bit gangly and not entirely able to coordinate her legs and paws. Her attempts to get over stiles were often comical and, more often than not, if we came to a gate she would wait for it to be opened for her. She was growing up.

'So,' said Adeline, 'this is what you and Teg are going to do. Send Teg to gather those sheep and bring them up to the gate at the other end of the hedge. You'll need to open the gate and stand above it to stop them going the wrong way up the lane. Teg then needs to drive the sheep down the lane and hold them at the next gate. You'll walk behind and when Teg stops them at the gate, you need to walk past them to open it and let them through. Teg will need to stop them bolting back up the lane. OK? Teg's had some practice at this and she's good at it. She won't need many commands, but when you do need to tell her something, make sure you are clear and confident.'

I had never undertaken anything as complicated as this before, but I could already see that Teg knew exactly what to do. We walked out into the field a bit closer to the sheep and I asked her to sit. She looked at me. 'Away!' I said. She didn't hesitate. She didn't go completely cleanly around the sheep, and missed a few, but on Adeline's instruction I told Teg to 'Get back' and she responded immediately, went around the stragglers and pushed them back to the main flock. She was moving fast and I was racing towards the gate at the top of the field so that Teg knew where I wanted the sheep brought to.

'Steady her up a bit,' called Adeline, 'she's going a bit quick.'

'Steady!' I managed, a little breathlessly, still running towards the gate, half backwards so I could keep an eye on the sheep.

'Tell her to stand, that'll slow them up.'

'Stand, Teg' and she did. She stopped. And the sheep slowed to an amble. I got to the gate and the sheep crowded around me. I made a bit of a mess of opening it and trying to get into position so that I could help Teg make sure the sheep went the right way, and at one point could swear that Teg was looking at me as if to say 'You know you're being a bit of an idiot, don't you?' She took charge and, with precious little useful help from me, got them all through the gate and moving quietly down the lane. I paused for a moment, just to enjoy the spectacle of a hundred or so retreating woolly bums being kept in check by a single ginger-and-white dog zigzagging behind them. As Adeline had trained her to do, Teg kept the sheep tight by the gate as I pushed through them to open it and not one tried to make a break for it and bolt back up the lane.

'You did well,' said Adeline.

'Teg did it all, really,' I said.

'But she listened to you, she worked for you.'

Adeline appears to have a sixth sense when it comes to animals. She can read sheep, dogs and horses in a way that is even more remarkable because she wasn't born on a farm. She got her first working dog when she was fifteen and had no one to tell her how to train it. She worked it out herself. But I was beginning to suspect that her sixth sense also extended to people. I think she was all too aware that I was on the brink of admitting defeat with Teg, although I have no idea how she would have known. And that afternoon, without ever saying the words, she had nonetheless told me not to give up. Teg and I didn't yet have that magical bond, we were a bit more Laurel and Hardy than Astaire and Rogers, but it didn't feel so completely out of reach any more.

'I think we should work towards getting her assessed by the Society,' said Adeline as we walked back to the house. 'If they pass her and we can find out more about her ancestry, we may be able to get her registered. I have a suspicion there's some Border Collie in there somewhere. If so, she can't be registered as pure Welsh, but let's see what we can find out.'

It would be entirely reasonable for you to ask what would be so bad about Teg having a Border Collie as an ancestor? Psychologist Stanley Coren's book *The Intelligence of Dogs* ranks Border Collies as the brightest of all the breeds. (In case you are wondering, Afghan Hounds win the prize for being the dimmest.) They excel at high-energy sports like flyball. They are so good at agility that no other breed stands a chance and to make the sport inclusive there are now ABC classes for Anything But a Collie. Biologist Ray Coppinger even trained one to be a sledge dog. Perro was a pet that belonged to Coppinger's statistics professor. If there is one thing Border Collies don't excel at, it is being pets. Perro spent his pent-up energy chasing cars, and the family, fearing for his safety, decided he would be better off in a new home. Coppinger put him as lead dog to a team of huskies. He was fast, super responsive to commands and he became what Coppinger described as his 'once in a lifetime dog'.

Another area where Border Collies dominate is search and rescue, although the idea of using dogs to find people dates back from a time before Border Collies existed. The earliest records of dogs being used to rescue lost or trapped people come from Switzerland. The Great St Bernard Hospice sits at 2,500 metres on the Great St Bernard Pass close to Switzerland's border with Italy. It was established in 1049 by an Italian archdeacon called – what else? – Bernard, to offer travellers over the mountains a safe refuge. Dogs are first mentioned in the archives from the late seventeenth century. These were most likely Swiss cattle dogs and other local breeds that were used to guard livestock, and would have been given to the monastery to protect both the monks and the travellers. The St Bernard Pass was a popular route, used by maybe as many as twenty thousand people a year – including, in 1800, Napoleon and his army. In winter it would have been treacherous, with deep snow and frequent avalanches, and the monks were often called on to help find people who had got lost or buried by an avalanche. The dogs would accompany them and proved to be very adept at not only navigating in thick fog or snowstorms, but at finding people buried deep in the snow. Later it was reported that the dogs would go out in small groups, without the monks, looking for lost people and if they found someone alive, one would go back to the hospice to raise the alarm while another would stay with the person they'd found to keep them warm.

Think of a St Bernard and you probably think of a huge, jowly, slobbery beast with a barrel of brandy around its neck. The brandy carrying was a myth – it never happened – and the first dogs of St Bernard were not quite so hefty, but they were hugely good at the job they had created for themselves and over the two hundred years they worked on the pass they are thought to have rescued around two thousand people. The last recorded rescue was in 1897. A twelve-year-old boy had fallen down a crevasse, was unconscious and almost dead. He was found and revived by a St Bernard – it was licking that did the trick according to one account I read – and lived to tell the tale. But the most famous St Bernard of all went by the unlikely name of Barry. He saved forty lives in his time, and when he died in 1814 he was stuffed and put on display in a museum in Berne. From that day to this, one dog at the hospice will always go by the name of Barry.

The dog credited with being Britain's first search-and-rescue dog was a mongrel that was seen wandering about the rubble and bombed-out buildings of East London after an air raid in 1940. Air Raid Warden Mr King took pity on the dog and threw him some scraps, little knowing that he had sparked the beginning of an extraordinary partnership. The dog stuck around and became something of a mascot for Mr King's civil defence team. They called him Rip and soon discovered that he had an amazing natural talent for finding people buried in collapsed buildings. His nose would start to twitch and he would dive into the rubble, his tail wagging, his paws frantically scrabbling away at the bricks. He saved over a hundred lives during the Blitz and he did it without any training at all. Rip's successes prompted the training of more dogs to find people in all the urban areas that were bombed during the war.

Still today, when disaster strikes a town or city anywhere in the world, dogs will be a vital part of the rescue effort. Perhaps the greatest challenge faced by modern day search-and-rescue teams was after the attack on the World Trade Center in New York on 11 September 2001. Three hundred dogs were drafted in to try and recover people – alive or dead – trapped in the debris. One of those dogs was Trakr. Trakr was a German Shepherd working with the Canadian Police Force. His handler, James Symington, was watching the events in New York unfold on television and knew he could do something to help. He and Trakr drove from their home in Nova Scotia to Manhattan – a journey of fifteen hours – getting to Ground Zero in the early hours of the morning of 12 September. By seven o'clock that same morning Trakr had found signs of life beneath the rubble. Genelle Guzman was buried under forty feet of concrete and had been there for twenty-six hours. She was the last of twenty people to be pulled out of the wreckage alive.

After World War Two the Swiss pioneered a more methodical approach to training dogs in mountain Search and Rescue techniques, but they didn't choose St Bernards, going instead for German Shepherds like Trakr, dogs known for their intelligence, agility, stamina and tremendous drive, which makes them easy to train. They proved to be a good choice and inspired Scottish mountaineer Hamish MacInnes, who brought techniques he'd seen used in the Alps back to the UK.

During his National Service in the late 1940s Hamish had spent time in the Tyrolean Mountains in Austria. He became friends with a mountain guide who was using his dogs to find people who had been buried by avalanches. When Hamish returned home to Glencoe in Scotland he decided to try and train his German Shepherds Tiki and Rangi to do the same. Glencoe and the Cairngorms had become the hubs for increasingly popular winter sports like skiing and climbing and, with no official mountain-rescue service in existence, when people got into trouble they had to rely on the kind-hearted, if inexpert, help of local police officers, gamekeepers and shepherds. Hamish wanted to establish a more formal, less haphazard service and believed dogs should be an integral part of it. His dogs both worked well and he gained further experience and inspiration when he attended an avalanche dog-training course training course with the Swiss Alpine Club. In the winter of 1964 he hosted a course of his own in Scotland for volunteers and their dogs, and their new-found skills were soon being put to the test. The movement grew and in the following year Hamish established the Search and Rescue Dog Association. It has been going ever since and has become a national institution working in England, Ireland and Wales as well as Scotland. German Shepherds are still used, as are other breeds like spaniels, Labradors and even good old mongrels, but today one breed dominates. Its image makes up the logo for the National Search and Rescue Dog Association. It is the Border Collie.

In 2001 I was at Heathrow to catch a flight to Delhi. In the departure lounge with me were a group of men and their dogs who were flying out to the beleaguered city of Gujarat which had been hit by a devastating earthquake a few days before. They were all Search and Rescue volunteers and were happy to chat and let me pet their dogs – all of them Border Collies. Brian Jones was with his dog Sian. I remember him being frustrated that the British Government hadn't organised for them to get to Gujarat sooner and was gloomily anticipating that they would only find dead bodies. Mercifully, that was not the case. He and Sian found thirty-eight people who were pulled out of the rubble alive.

But of all their talents, it is their herding abilities that have made Border Collies a firm favourite with sheep farmers the world over. The breed is actually a relatively new one that originates, as the name leads you to suspect, from the Scottish Borders. Their ancestors would have been, like the Welsh sheepdog, not so much a breed as a good working type with strong herding instincts and the necessary strength and stamina to control the animals and cope with the terrain. Through selective breeding they developed the traits that make Border Collies so distinctive today; they work low to the ground, almost stalking the sheep, and they work silently, relying on intimidating the sheep with their fixed stare. Unlikely though it sounds, it is a very effective method, as all viewers of *One Man and His Dog* know.

Sheepdog trials started in 1873 and would probably have been very similar to one I went to in Mid Wales one weekend in the early autumn of 2015. I arrived at a wild and distant spot in the mountains after a spectacular three-hour drive, most of it on single-track lanes. A few Land Rovers and pick-ups were already there, parked at jaunty angles on a steep hillside. Tea, homemade ham sandwiches and Welsh cakes were being served from a caravan and everyone there had a Welsh dog either wandering beside them or sitting in the back of their truck. It was very much a Welsh Sheepdog Society affair with the atmosphere of a large family picnic. Adeline, her husband Tim and daughter Oonagh were all there. The competition was between teams from North, Mid and South Wales and Adeline was competing with Smasher for the South Wales team. Teg and I were not competing, although Adeline and I had agreed it was something we could aspire to. When I saw what the dogs were going to have to do, I knew I'd be aspiring for quite some time.

The course was quite unlike anything I had ever seen. For a start we weren't in a field but on a mountain. From where we were parked the land dropped away into a steep-sided valley with a single-track road and a stream running along the bottom. The land then rose steeply up on the other side, a jumble of bracken and bog and rock, to another high point, where just about visible was a small flock of sheep. Each dog would have to make their way up to the sheep – a distance of almost a mile – gather them up and drive them off the hill, over the road and back up to where their handler would be waiting. At that point the second member of the team with their dog would take over and drive the sheep into a set of pens, split them up and load half of them in a trailer and then get them out again.

I bought a cup of tea and Teg and I joined the little gathering on the bank to watch the action. It was clear from the outset that this was a challenging course for both dogs and handlers. Dogs working on their home turf with sheep they know is one thing, but having to work dogs with sheep they don't know across unfamiliar terrain is quite another. And the distances they were having to cover were far greater than those in a standard sheepdog trial. It was amazing to watch, but it was also easy to understand why in the late 1890s farmers had their heads turned by the arrival of a new dog that amused and bemused the spectators in equal measure. The first records of it were at a sheepdog trial in Bala, North Wales, when a dog was reported to herd the sheep 'by creeping and crawling' – the classic, rather showy style of the Border Collie. The Welsh style of working is efficient, practical and impressive but in a way that is more low-key and less obvious. The Border Collie is a crowd-pleaser and by the 1930s anyone who wanted to compete in trials wanted to do it with one of these new dogs. After the war they became even more desirable and young farmers started to choose the stylish and, by now, fashionable Border Collies, not just to work but to cross-breed with their existing Welsh dogs to create an excellent hybrid.

John Davies was one of the judges I met on the trial day. He farms in a beautiful part of Mid Wales just inland from Aberystwyth and comes from a long line of Welsh farmers. His great-grandfather was one of the last drovers, the men who were responsible for driving livestock often huge distances across the country from farms to markets. He not only worked with Welsh dogs, but also became renowned as a breeder. Three generations later John is carrying on that family tradition, but back in 1997 made an alarming discovery. He was looking for a dog to breed with his Welsh bitch Topsy but all the local farms now had Border Collies or cross breeds. He contacted Huw Thomas. Huw was then the livestock commissioner for Wales and his job required him to travel around all the farms in the country. John asked him if he could help him track down a Welsh dog fit for breeding anywhere in Wales. Huw started to ask around and his search found only eighty pure-bred Welsh dogs and of those fewer than thirty were young enough to breed. The Border Collie, famed for saving lives, had pushed the magnificent Welsh sheepdog, so intrinsic to life in rural Wales for well over a thousand years, to the brink of extinction.

When the perilous state of the Welsh sheepdog came to light, Huw and John established the Welsh Sheepdog Society with the aim of preserving and promoting the breed. It has had some success and there are now two thousand registered Welsh sheepdogs. I hoped that one day Teg might be allowed to join this rather elite group, if Adeline's suspicions were wrong and we could prove she had no Border Collie ancestors. And that was not going to be straightforward. Bronwen had told me she had bred Missy with a very handsome fellow by the name of Cymroy. Cymroy belongs to a charming man called Henry Alexander who lives on a small farm right on the edge of the town of Llantrisant. An accident a few years earlier had left him a bit less mobile and he sold most of his sheep and cattle, but he still keeps a few for Cymroy to work with, and, as I saw when Henry invited me to come and meet him, Cymroy is also very adept at rounding up ducks and chickens. Although there was little resemblance between him and Teg, the resemblance to Teg's brother Taff was very strong indeed. Adeline looked him up on her Society records. She found out that not only is he registered but he comes from a very distinguished line that goes all the way back to John Davies's Topsy. Topsy, it transpires, was Teg's great-great-grandmother.

'That makes you almost royalty!' I said to Teg, who gave me a slightly imperious look by way of response. So there was no doubt that one side of Teg's ancestry would pass the rigorous requirements of the Society, but when it came to trying to find out more about her mother's side, it proved to be rather trickier.

In 2008 Bronwen was working for a farmer in Cheshire. She had gone there for a month to help with lambing and while she was there, he asked her if she could go and pick up a puppy for him. He had bought the puppy from a farmer just over the border in North Wales and Bronwen arranged to meet him in a lay-by on the Horseshoe Pass. In the back of his truck was the dog pup Bronwen's employer had bought, and a second pup, a bitch.

'She was such a sweet little thing,' Bronwen told me.

'I'd never seen anything like her. She looked just like a little fox.'

Bronwen grew up working with sheep and dogs but her father always had Border Collies. She knew nothing about Welsh dogs, 'but I couldn't leave that puppy on her own, so I took her too.' She wasn't registered, didn't have any papers, but Bronwen wasn't worried about that. 'She turned out to be one of the best dogs I have ever worked with and she's a great mum. She has lovely puppies, as you know!'

'Is there any chance you can remember the name of the farmer you bought her from?'

Bron looked doubtful. 'It was a long time ago. I might be able to find the name of the man I was working for and we could maybe track him down that way. The problem is I'm about to move house. Everything is in boxes. I'll see what I can do, but it is going to take a while.'

There was, I assured her, no rush, because even if Teg's ancestry could be traced all the way back to the days of Hywel Dda, if she didn't pass the assessment, she still couldn't be registered. And I had a lot more practice to put in before I was willing to let my precious dog be scrutinised by the super-critical eyes of the Society assessors.

Chapter 10
Brothers In Arms

Fire with WO1 Dodds

Histories are more full of examples of the fidelities of dogs than of friends.

Alexander Pope, English poet, in a letter to
Henry Cromwell

We live at the dead end of a steep forestry track, all rocks and potholes with a couple of hairpin bends thrown in for good measure. The only people who venture up it are lost or are trying to get to our house. When our friend Jamie first came to visit, he climbed out of his truck looking a little shaky and said, 'Do you just hate people?' The noise of protesting engines and hasty gear changes can be heard well in advance of any vehicle's arrival, and prompts a response from my dogs that their ancient ancestors would have been proud of. They break into a cacophony of barking and, if the door is open, rush out looking as threatening as two small scruffy mongrels and a permanently smiling sheepdog can look. It is very useful for us, as we have no doorbell, but a little intimidating for anyone who hasn't been before. The postman, Keith, is entirely used to it and opens the door of his van to be greeted by wagging tails, muddy paws and the hopeful expectation that he might have some treats in the glove compartment.

Colonel Smith braved the track and arrived, immaculate in military fatigues, highly polished boots and a beret worn at what I imagine is a carefully regimented angle. He let his equally immaculate black Labrador out of the boot of his car just as my dogs rushed out to give them both the once over. They were less than welcoming. Teg pulled herself up to her full height, tail aloft, and stood over the slightly cowering Lab, like a bouncer threatening an underage teenager trying to get into a club. Bella pulled back her upper lips, revealing her teeth and snarled. Badger turned his back on her and peed copiously on Colonel Smith's back tyre.

'Good God, dogs, show some respect!' And they were court-martialled and shut in the boot room.

'Sorry,' I said, returning, mortified, to my visitor. 'I don't think I've ever met a colonel before and I'm not sure that was the appropriate way to greet you. Should I salute, or curtsey or something?'

'No, but you can make me a cup of coffee.'

Colonel 'call me Neil' Smith is in the RAVC – or Royal Army Veterinary Corps. Military personnel, I was to discover, speak almost entirely in acronyms. The Army Veterinary Service (as it was originally known) was founded in 1796 because the British public were outraged that so many Army horses were dying, not, as it turns out, as a direct result of combat, but because they weren't being looked after properly. The British Army wasn't using dogs at the time, although dogs have been used in battle for – well, probably since the very start of our partnership. 'Put that mammoth bone down, or I'll set my wolf on you . . .' Certainly the Ancient Greeks and Romans used heavy mastiff-type dogs wearing collars adorned with sharp metal spikes, just to add a little extra something to the teeth and claws. The Romans also used their dogs as messengers and it was in this role that dogs first came to prominence in more modern British warfare.

Author Rebecca Frankel in her book *War Dogs* tells the remarkable story of Lieutenant Colonel E. H. Richardson who in 1914 petitioned the British Army to add dogs to its ranks. His fascination with military dogs began early in his career. While visiting friends in the Scottish Highlands he came across a man who was procuring Border Collies on behalf of the German Government. Intrigued, Richardson went to Germany and saw how the Germans were training 'ambulance' dogs to find wounded men in battlefields. He decided to try it himself and added a collie called Sanita to his already extensive collection of dogs at home. Together with his wife and the help of friends, neighbours and local schoolchildren playing the parts of injured soldiers, he set about training the dogs, both as ambulance dogs and messenger dogs. He knew how invaluable they could be and many of his fellow officers saw it too. They wrote to the War Office. They received no response.

Meanwhile Colonel Richardson was supplying ambulance and messenger dogs to other armies all over the world, including Russia, India, Turkey and Spain. He would go with the dogs, and over the years he garnered a wealth of knowledge about how foreign armies used their dogs, and adopted some of the ideas himself.

Come 1914 and the outbreak of war, he knew that allies and enemies alike would be using military dogs on the front line – Germany, Italy, Russia, Sweden and the Netherlands all used military dogs, but the War Office was not to be persuaded. Undeterred, he wrote to Battersea Dogs Home asking for lurchers, Airedales, collies, sheepdogs and whippets. It was these dogs that he thought would be most suited to the battlefield, and after six weeks' training he had ambulance and messenger dogs ready to go to the front. The government still refused to accept his offer, and he gave the dogs to the British Red Cross and other allied forces. Very quickly the dogs proved their worth. He continued to lobby anyone who would listen and even wrote a letter to the *New York Times* in 1915 stating, 'The Germans have recognised the value that dogs were likely to be in battle. [Germany had about six thousand military dogs.] It is a pity that the value of these dogs has not been generally recognised by the French and English Armies.'

It wasn't until 1916 that the first of Richardson's dogs went to the front line. Two Airedales, Prince and Wolf, were sent to France to an officer in the Royal Artillery who wanted messenger dogs to carry notes between the main unit and his outpost. They were a huge success, and Richardson was flooded with requests for more dogs. Throughout the remainder of the war, the dogs Richardson trained and sent to the army saved thousands of lives and many also lost their own lives in the line of duty. Jack was an Airedale Terrier whose battalion was surrounded by German soldiers. They had no supplies and no means of communication. Jack was sent with a message attached to his collar with an urgent request for help. Amid a barrage of enemy fire, which smashed his jaw, ripped open his back and shattered one of his legs, Jack made it to headquarters to deliver the message that saved his battalion. He died from his injuries.

The Americans had been similarly resistant to having dogs as part of their military capability and the dog who served with the 102nd Infantry Regiment shouldn't have been there at all. He was a stray dog, described as a 'Boston Terrier', which looks a bit like a Staffie, and was found wandering around the regiment's training grounds. One of the men, Corporal Robert Conroy, adopted the dog, named him Stubby, and smuggled him on board the troop ship that was taking them all to France. The story goes that when Stubby was discovered by the commanding officer, Stubby saluted him, as the soldiers had trained him to do, and he was allowed to stay on board.

He entered combat on 5 February 1918 and served with

the regiment in the trenches of northern France, where he was poisoned by mustard gas and injured twice by grenade. He learnt to warn his unit of gas attacks and incoming artillery shells, found injured men on the battlefield and captured a German spy. He was nominated for the rank of sergeant, and was awarded three medals. Both he and Robert Conroy survived and Conroy smuggled Stubby home where he was hailed as a hero.

Military Working Dogs have served with the British Army in every major conflict since. They have proved invaluable in all sorts of terrain and in various theatres of war, from jungles to deserts to cities, in Borneo, Kenya, Kosovo, Northern Ireland, Iraq and most recently in Afghanistan. Over the years their role has changed and developed. Today dogs are used for protection, guarding military installations and giving warning to troops on the ground of ambush attacks or suicide bombers. In jungle warfare they are used as trackers, but probably the most vital role they play is as detection dogs. And it was this extraordinary talent that dogs have that helped Neil decide on his career.

Settled in the kitchen with his dog at his side and a cup of coffee, Neil told me how a school visit to the RAVC centre at Melton Mowbray mapped out his future. 'It was hearing what man and dog could do together, about the amazing finds, taking weapons and explosives off the streets in Northern Ireland, that did it.' He heard an incredible story of a handler and his dog going in to search a house because it was suspected there were weapons in there. Nothing was found but the dog kept indicating at a plastered wall so persistently that they decided to have a look. They dug through the plaster and found a pistol, which, from the age of the plaster, they guessed had been there for at least twenty-five years. Another team had been searching a field and a dog indicated that there was something buried. The soldiers got their metal detectors out, dug around at the spot but found nothing. The handler was so convinced that his dog was on to something that he sneaked back later with his own shovel. He dug down five or six feet and found a rusty lump. It was a musket, probably from the Battle of the Boyne era and buried for over three hundred years. 'And I thought, this is really interesting,' said Neil, 'and it was that that spurred me on to join up – only for four years, though.'

'And how long have you been in the RAVC now?'

'Twenty-six years.'

Neil did two tours in Northern Ireland working alongside Military Working Dog handlers. 'They were such a great bunch of people. And every day they would go out and look for bombs. Every day. That's quite a challenging job.'

Every war is different, every one presents new and different challenges for the Military Working Dogs. Throughout the recent war in Afghanistan the method of warfare and the tactics employed changed constantly. Most significantly it saw the development of a particularly effective and deadly weapon: the Improvised Explosive Device or IED.

Neil's dog (named somewhat incongruously, Fire) was an IED detection dog in Afghanistan. IED dogs work with a handler and accompany infantry patrols. The job of the dog is to walk in front of the patrol, checking for any IEDs. IEDs are often tiny, very well hidden and contain few, if any, metal parts, so can't be picked up by metal detectors. The majority of casualties and fatalities that happened as a result of the war in Afghanistan were caused by IEDs. If the dog detects one it is trained to stop and indicate where it is. Then the bomb disposal unit will be called in to disable it. Unfortunately for Fire, a device she found went off. Neil showed me some photographs. 'She had a fractured jaw, a fracture under her eye, a bit of the bomb went right through her metacarpals and she had quite a lot of skin loss and tissue loss down one side.' She was medically evacuated to Camp Bastion, given emergency treatment by vets there and then flown back to the UK where she was nursed back to health.

'It does seem extraordinary,' I said, 'that a dog with injuries like Fire's isn't just put down. Surely that is the practical thing to do?'

'Well, the welfare of the animal comes first. The vets there were optimistic she would make a good recovery and these dogs are part of the team. Not only that, they are very, very good for morale. They are treated exactly the same as a wounded soldier.'

Once the British military was persuaded that dogs had an important and vital role to play in World War Two, it swiftly transpired that dogs, as well as performing their duties carrying messages and finding wounded soldiers on the battlefield, had an enormously positive effect on the mental wellbeing of the troops. In Simon's Town on the Cape Peninsula in South Africa there is a big naval base and outside it is a statue of a Great Dane, standing on a rock, a seaman's cap at his feet. When I first saw it, I assumed it was a memorial to a loyal dog that had waited at that spot day and night for his master, who had been lost at sea. That wasn't the case at all. The dog – called Just Nuisance – was exactly that, a nuisance. He took a liking to the sailors and would hang around the naval base, usually on the top of gangplanks where he was in everyone's way. He would also follow the sailors on the train to neighbouring suburbs and even in to Cape Town, much to their delight. But the railway company was not amused; unless he paid his fare – or someone paid it for him – he would have to be stopped from using the trains or be put down. The sailors petitioned the Navy to do something to save the dog and, unlikely though it sounds, the Navy came up with a brilliant plan. They enlisted Just Nuisance as an Ordinary Seaman, which meant he was entitled to free train travel. Later he was promoted to Able Seaman which gave him rations and a cap. It seems a wildly eccentric thing for the Navy to do, but as a morale booster for the troops he was irreplaceable.

Fire was retired in 2012 and Neil adopted her as a pet, but she has since become something of a poster girl. She was the mascot for the British team at the Invictus Games and stood in to receive a Dickin Medal – one that is awarded to animals that have displayed 'conspicuous gallantry or devotion to duty while serving or associated with any branch of the Armed Forces or Civil Defence Units'. The medal had been awarded posthumously to another IED detection dog, Sasha. In her time in

Afghanistan Sasha had fifteen confirmed finds of IEDs, mortars and hidden weaponry, saving the lives of countless soldiers and civilians. She and her handler Lance Corporal Kenneth Rowe were considered the best team working in the Kandahar region. They were both killed in an ambush by a rocket-propelled grenade.

Throughout our conversation Fire had been lying patiently at Neil's feet, but when I went to replenish his coffee she got up and nudged at his elbow. He stroked her. 'Yes, hello, we're talking about you.' A few minutes later she came and nudged him again, but he was showing me photographs and ignored her. She walked to the other end of the table, squatted and peed copiously on the floor. 'It's revenge!' I laughed. 'Retaliation for my dogs being so unwelcoming. Shall we take them all for a walk?'

After a flurry of emails, phone calls and a meeting at a barracks in Surrey to assess my requirements, I was given permission to visit the RAVC training centre in Melton Mowbray. There I met Jay Rowlinson, the Officer Commanding of the canine training squadron. He coordinates the training of both dogs and handlers for detection and protection work. The use of IEDs in the latter part of the war in Afghanistan kept Jay particularly busy. Dogs had proved to be so useful that they became an UOR. I looked at him questioningly. '"An Urgent Operational Requirement". At the height of the conflict there was a dog and handler available for every single infantry section that worked out of the wire [outside the base]. Whenever a patrol went out they had the opportunity to take a dog and the majority of them did.'

I was surprised that dogs still played such a key role, when the military spends a huge amount of time and resources constantly developing and honing technology and equipment. Haven't they managed to come up with something that can better a dog?

Jay shook his head. 'The dog's nose is a million times better than anything out there. Not only that, a dog can think for itself, which no machine can at this stage. And a dog can work almost out of sight of command. If it can find a device as far away from the handler and the rest of the patrol as possible, that is better and safer for all involved. But the key really is that the dog is incredibly adaptable. To advance technology takes a long time. If they change the component parts of an IED, it will take months to develop the technology to find those new parts. For a dog it is just a case of learning a new scent. It can do that in about five days.'

How, I wondered, do you go about training a dog to find explosives, particularly ones that are of no set design and can be made of any number of different materials? Jay told me the dogs are taught to indicate on component parts, like battery packs, pressure plates and wires, for which they are rewarded with praise and usually a play with their favourite toy like a tennis ball. But they have also discovered that dogs appear to have the capacity to recognise and understand when a scent might be out of context or wrong, even if they haven't been trained on that particular scent.

Private Rob Purchase did two tours of Afghanistan working with three separate battalions, and a dog and handler went out on every single patrol. The first troop commander he went out with expressed a certain amount of scepticism about how useful the dog would prove to be, 'but,' said Rob, 'as soon as you have your first find and they see the dog does actually work, they always want to go out with a dog. It's a confidence booster, especially when you have a dog like Harvey who would work up to two hundred and fifty metres in front of the patrol.'

Harvey was a black Labrador – 'a monster, to put it politely, but we had such a good relationship, a real bond.' Rob and Harvey worked with each other for over six months – were never apart, even, sometimes, when it came to sleeping. If they were in some small patrol base out in the middle of nowhere there was often no room for Harvey, so everyone would get together to build him a small hut and Rob would sleep in there too. Having a dog with them gave people what Rob described as a 'sense of home' – it was good to have a dog around, something to play with, and if it had been a bad day, Rob said, Harvey was the perfect tonic. 'Who can't smile at a dog wagging its tail, jumping all over the place, just so happy to be alive?'

'Can you remember your first find?' I asked.

They were out on patrol on the outskirts of a village. They had had reports from the locals that the Taliban had been active in the area and were going out to make sure it was safe for people to move around. As they approached a compound the Patrol Commander asked Rob to send in Harvey. 'As soon as he reached the wall, his behaviour changed. His nose hit the bottom of the wall and he searched along the length of it until he got to a stack of corn. Then he just lay down.' Harvey had found a wire leading along the length of the wall and into the stack of corn where it was connected to a fifteen-kilo DFD. 'Directional Fragmentation Device,' Rob added quickly when I looked at him blankly. 'It was a barrel filled with nails, old screws, bolts, with explosives at the bottom of it, so it's going to hurt.' It's going to do a lot more than that. Harvey had saved dozens of lives.

'And how do you reward him when he finds something like that? Presumably you can't start chucking tennis balls around?'

'No, you just give them lots of praise and a bit of fuss, but then when we got back to base I would give him a bit more training and reward him with the tennis ball, just to reiterate to him that he'd done good.'

Anyone reading this who has a dog must feel the same as I do, that it must be incredibly difficult to put a dog with which you have such a strong bond into a potentially life-threatening situation. But, as Rob explained, the bond is really the key. 'It's having that bond, that confidence in the dog to think "This dog is good enough. He won't miss it". But if something bad did happen, it would knock me for six. It would knock anyone for six.'

Lance Corporal Chris Slack knows only too well what it is like when something bad happens. On his second operational tour in Afghanistan he was working with his dog Oddy in High Assurance Search. HAS dogs work in areas where intelligence has identified a known threat. 'You know there's something there, you just don't know where it is.' About a week into the tour Chris and Oddy went out with a search team to a compound the Taliban had been using. It was, Chris said, a massive compound and he and another handler were tasked to go in and search it. The dogs work meticulously over small areas at a time. They will be sent just a few metres away from the handler, search that area, return to the handler, be sent forward another few metres and so on. It is painstaking and incredibly dangerous. Chris and Oddy started outside the compound and then moved inside, searching just a metre or so at a time. Chris spotted a white flag – the Taliban flag – flying in the middle of the compound. He knew it could be a trap. 'They are renowned for putting IEDs under the white flag 'cos the squaddies would go in, grab the flag and pull it down.' He sent Oddy on, just a few metres, and then he is not sure what happened. 'There was a little flicker in the corner. I don't know if there was a lizard or something, but it made her jump and all of a sudden an IED went off.'

Chris had worked with Oddy for eight months. 'There was nothing in the back of my mind thinking "Shit! What if something happens?" A HAS dog has never been killed, so I thought it just wouldn't happen.' But it did. When the IED went off Oddy was blown up.

'It's a blur to me,' says Chris. 'The Engineer Searcher who was with me said I was screaming out her name. He had to stop me running to her, but there was nothing left of her. Everything there is out to test you, to kill you. Oddy was my best friend.' But despite what had happened, just two weeks later Chris was back out working again with another dog called Fanta.

'I shouldn't have done that really, because it affected me in the long run, but I needed to prove to myself and to others that I could do it; I could do the job.'

'Did you feel like you'd screwed up?'

'Yes, massively.'

'You felt responsible?'

'Yes, definitely. I still do now.'

Chris worked with Fanta until the end of the tour. She was, he said, 'a lovely little dog, a brilliant personality', but he knew he wasn't working her properly. 'It was constantly on my mind, what had happened. I knew she could do more, but I didn't want to put her in danger.' Someone told me later that Chris had been one of the best handlers, but he couldn't come to terms with what had happened. He was referred to a psychiatrist, but told me that speaking about his experiences hadn't helped. 'It's just me. I've got to deal with it. It's constant . . .'

'Has it made you question the use of dogs by the military?'

'Oh God, no, no. They love doing their job and they are very good at what they do, but I can't see them as equipment now. It might sound bad, but I'd rather see a person get it, than a dog.'

Chris's experience was traumatic, but mercifully uncommon. Most Military Working Dogs retire and get rehomed. Harvey, in Rob's words, 'is now living life in front of the fire with some civilian'. Fire, of course, now enjoys celebrity status with Neil and then there's Joey.

Joey worked with Lance Corporal Victoria Emberson as a Vehicle Search dog for seven months after spending a month together training at Melton Mowbray. 'We were pretty much inseparable. We spent a lot of time together.'

Joey is not your typical Military Working Dog. Most of them are spaniels or Labradors, Belgian Malinois or German Shepherds, but Joey's ancestry is uncertain. Vicki laughed. 'He's not the best-looking dog in the world, so people thought I'd just got a stray and trained it up. But he turned out to be one of the best Vehicle Search dogs of his tour. He was also my comfort blanket.'

Vicki was one of only two women at the forward operating base where she was stationed. 'It's quite daunting when you arrive. No one talks to you much. They are quite stand-offish, so having Joey with me made me feel a lot better and less lonely.'

At the end of the tour Vicki realised that Joey wasn't doing quite so well. 'They're not robots. He was eight years old by then and had stopped being himself. I realised he was potentially coming to the end of his career.'

She put a letter in to advise her superiors and to ask if she could rehome him when the time came. She was then sent to Cyprus for two years and Joey went to the British military base in Germany. Just as she was leaving Cyprus, Vicki was told that Joey was up for rehoming. 'It wasn't ideal because it was going to cost me a thousand pounds to fly him home from Germany, which was my entire savings, but . . .'

Joey is now fourteen, pretty much blind, almost deaf, but clearly devoted to Vicki whose side he never left throughout the time I was with her.

Back with Jay Rowlinson, I asked about the future.

Everyone is aware that there have been huge spending cuts which have seen the army reduced from 150,000 people when Jay joined thirty years ago to roughly 82,000 now. But the RAVC has grown to three times the size it was in the same time, solely thanks to the success the dogs have proven to be. At the height of operations in Afghanistan there were one hundred and twelve dog teams working out there. Currently the demand for dogs is outstripping the RAVC's ability to supply them, but, Jay warned, they can't afford to be complacent.

Major Rebecca Hart's job is to look ahead and plan for future conflicts, deciding what to focus on with regards to requirements and training. 'We need to stay on top of demand and on top of the game.' One of the ways they are doing that is training dogs to do two jobs instead of one.

'When you go somewhere new,' Beccy explained, 'you can only take as many people as will fit in an aircraft or on a ship and you need as much flexibility as possible, so a dog that can do two things rather than one doubles their capabilities.'

Many of the new dogs will be trained in protection and detection, whereas before they would be trained in one or the other. 'Have you seen *Black Hawk Down?*' Jay asked me.

I shook my head. 'A bit boysy for me,' I confessed.

'It is, but that's how I see dogs working in the future – in Somalia, in Syria, in the thick of it. You're heading somewhere and you put your dog into search mode, then you walk around a corner and there's a suicide bomber coming at you, or someone's pointing an AK-47 and you send your dog in to attack and take them out. The chips are down. A metal detector won't work, lots of other technology won't work, but dogs will.'

Chapter 11
Follow Me

Marjory and Mouse

Dogs are better than human beings because they know, but they do not tell.

Emily Dickinson, American poet, in a letter to
Thomas Wentworth Higginson

On Morristown Green in New Jersey, among Civil War statues of George Washington meeting the Marquis de Lafayette and Alexander Hamilton, and a sentimental portrayal of a man leaving his wife, baby and teenage son to head off to fight the British, is a more modern sculpture of a man wearing a suit and walking a German Shepherd. It commemorates an event that happened over eighty years ago in a completely different town altogether.

Dorothy Eustis was a wealthy American philanthropist based in Switzerland in the 1920s where she bred and trained German Shepherds for the army, police and customs. She came across a guide-dog training school in Berlin for war veterans. The gas attacks used against soldiers on all sides during World War One had devastating effects on those that survived them. Many came home blinded, the visual world lost to them for ever. Now there was a new way for the human–dog relationship to be utilised: guiding.

Dorothy wrote an article about the guide-dog training school for a popular American magazine. In response she received a storm of letters, including one from Morris Frank, a twenty-year-old from Nashville, Tennessee. His mother, Jessie, was blind – caused by two unrelated accidents – and Morris was her guide and helper. Then, by strange coincidence, Morris lost his sight, also thanks to two unrelated accidents. He was out riding his horse at the age of sixteen when he hit a low-hanging branch and was blinded in one eye. He lost the sight in his second eye in a boxing match with a friend. Morris heard about Dorothy's article – which was entitled 'The Seeing Eye' – and wrote to her asking, 'Is what you say really true? If so, I want one of those dogs! And I am not alone. Thousands of blind like me abhor being dependent on others. Help me and I will help them. Train me and I will bring my dog back and show people here how a blind man can be absolutely on his own.'

Dorothy took up the challenge. In the February of 1928 she called Morris and invited him to her dog-training school in Switzerland. Working with her at this time was another American, Jack Humphrey, and it was Jack who was given the task of training Morris to work with a dog. Morris was paired with a female German Shepherd who he renamed Buddy, and just a few months later he returned to New York with Buddy and Jack to tell anyone who would listen that this dog had changed his life. To prove it, he gave sceptical reporters a demonstration of Buddy's abilities by crossing Broadway unscathed during the evening rush hour.

Less than a year after Morris had travelled to Switzerland he established the Seeing Eye, the first guide-dog training school in America. The story came to the attention of two British women who were German Shepherd enthusiasts, and they contacted Dorothy to see if she wanted to extend her work to the UK. Dorothy agreed and sent over William Debetaz, one of her trainers. A piece of land and a garage were rented in Wallasey and the first partnerships in Britain between a blind person and a dog were established. One of the earliest beneficiaries was Allen Caldwell, who wrote, 'Not only has my dog given me glorious freedom and independence, never known since the war days, but delightful companionship.'

But how do you go about training a dog to 'see' for its owner? Dogs' eyes work differently from our own and, although dogs are superior to us in so many ways, eyesight isn't one of them. Dogs can't see the full range of colours we can, and although their low-light vision is better than ours, they cannot see as well at a distance, or indeed, objects that are very close up. I've often noticed this when playing Frisbee with Badger and Bella. The Frisbee is red – a colour dogs see as dark grey, so to them it will not stand out against green grass as much as it does for me. Not only that, if it has flown way over their heads and landed out of sight, they often struggle to find it. Sometimes they will be so close it is almost literally under their noses. They can smell it, but they can't see it.

This conundrum gave me the perfect excuse to get in contact with my old friend Penny. Fifteen years or so ago I was walking down a London street when a phone started ringing. Mobile phones were still a relatively new phenomenon then and although as someone working freelance I was absolutely expected to have one, I resented using it, so it took me a while to realise that the irritating ringing phone was, in fact, mine.

'Hello,' I said, sounding flustered and shouting over the traffic.

'Hello,' said a voice on the other end of the phone. 'Is that Kate Humble?'

I confirmed it was.

'My name is Dr Penny Allen and I'm calling from the

BBC Natural History Unit. I just wanted to check. You're a diver, aren't you?'

The upshot of this phone call was that Penny and I went to work in the Cayman Islands together in the hope of capturing the rarely seen and little-known six-gill shark on film. After spending many hours several hundred metres underwater in very small submarines with nothing more than a ziplock bag should our bladders fail us, we were either going to hate each other or become firm friends. Happily it proved to be the latter.

But then some years later Penny did the unthinkable. She sold her flat in Bristol, packed up her stuff and left the BBC for good. 'I'd been at the BBC for thirteen years and I did some amazing projects and really enjoyed it, but I do think it's quite a young person's job. There's a lot of travel involved, you spend a lot of time away from home, there's a lot of stress, long hours. I think I just realised that I wanted to do something that was more for me, kind of more personally rewarding, certainly less stressful, something that made me smile every day.'

Although Penny had spent almost her entire professional life working with animals, it was, she said 'too remote; there was no real contact with them'. She felt her future would be happier if she was working with dogs. I was intrigued. Why was this woman, who had spent years seeking out and studying animals that are exotic and extraordinary, rare and inaccessible being drawn to an animal that is so widespread and familiar?

'We'd always had pet dogs and I'd always been really close to them. It's funny, I was reading an article not that long ago about how a lot of children turn to dogs instead of their siblings for emotional support, and I think I was probably one of those kids. If I'd had a bad day at school I'd go and hug the Labrador rather than tell anyone else about it. So I think for me it was that connection to dogs in particular that made me want to work with them.'

She saw a job advertised for a guide-dog trainer and her first thought was, 'I didn't even know that job existed!' Penny is meticulous about most things, and her approach to finding her new career was no different. She read up, she researched and the more she found out about the job the more she wanted to do it. She applied and the job was hers.

Penny has been at the Forfar Guide Dog Training Centre near Aberdeen for the last six years. 'Can I come and see what you do?' I texted.

'Yes! Bring walking boots and warm stuff. I know it's warm down south but it is still like the depths of winter up here. Let me know when your flight gets in.'

Penny drove us to the centre the next morning in bright sunshine and in between shedding my wintry layers I asked her how you train to become a guide-dog trainer.

'Well, it's quite a long process, it takes over a year. There's a little bit of classroom work, but it is very much on-the-job training and we do everything with positive reinforcement techniques. It is based on the theory that if a dog or any animal finds an experience pleasurable it's more likely to repeat it; if they find something really unpleasant they're less likely to repeat it. So every time a dog does something that we want it to do, say stopping and sitting at a kerb edge, we reward it with a treat or a cuddle, depending on what motivates the dog more; then they're more likely to do that again.'

I asked when she first started working with dogs.

'Oh, pretty much straightaway. I was matched up with a tutor and given initially just two dogs. You start doing basic obedience with them, just lead work, making sure that you've got control of the dog and it's listening to you and developing that bond that's so important in learning later on. My first two were black Lab Retriever crosses. They were actually brothers called Quin and Quest, but they couldn't have been more different. It was a brilliant example of how you can have dogs from the same litter that have totally different temperaments and totally different handling styles.'

Just like Taff and Teg, I thought.

'Quin was quite reserved and sensitive and he needed quite a lot of confidence building and so a very supportive handling approach. Whereas his brother, Quest, was incredibly cheeky, bouncy and energetic, quite challenging at times. He always had a mischievous nature and his favourite game was to steal things and run off with them – he's been known to parade around with tea towels, slippers and even the occasional item of underwear!'

When Teg is working well and I remember the right instructions to give her and the sheep move in the direction I want them to, I get an inkling of what it is like to have formed a true working partnership and bond with a dog. It is a euphoric feeling that makes me want to turn cartwheels.

But the truth is, if it is a day when things don't go right and my lack of skill and Teg's lack of experience mean that the sheep stay where they are for another day or so, it's not the end of the world. For someone visually impaired, the working partnership between them and their dog can't ever be one that is haphazard or has an element of surprise. And once you come to rely on the support of a dog, life without one becomes almost untenable.

When Penny and I had been planning my visit, she wrote, 'If you want to get a really good sense of the partnership that forms between a guide-dog owner and their dog, I'll introduce you to Marjory.'

Marjory Hughes works on reception at Forfar. She is a little formidable, enormously efficient, and, Penny told me, the whole place would go to pot without her. Marjory was born unsighted. Her parents, though, treated her no differently from her sighted siblings. 'What they did, I did,' she told me as we sat with our tea in one of the meeting rooms at the centre. 'I even drove the car. My dad took my brothers and sisters out for driving lessons and he took me one time and he says, "Are you coming over to the estate to have a lesson?" I went, "Yeah," and my mum's like, "You can't do that, Harry," and he went, "Yeah, I can."'

But Marjory's mother didn't like dogs, so Marjory's pleas for a pet were always turned down. At the age of twenty, Marjory came up with a plan. She would apply for a guide dog. Her mother couldn't refuse her a dog then. Khan arrived just before her twenty-first birthday and was, she described, 'the best present ever'. But, I wondered, given that she had lived what appeared to be a very full and pretty independent life up to that point, did having a dog really make a noticeable difference?

'Definitely. Well, I could go out on my own and I didn't have a long cane to trip people up with and knock into lamp posts and stuff. I didn't have to ask anybody to pick me up from anywhere or come with me or take me to this place or that place. And when I got my first dog I remember saying to my dad, "Oh, do you know, the gas board are always digging up the streets?" and he said, "Oh, I know," and I went, "How do you know?" And he went, "Oh, well, OK, I'll let you into a little secret. For the last six months I've been following you to work and back from work. I didn't trust the dog, I didn't trust that he could help you. I didn't want you to know that I was following you, and usually you're so quick to pick things up, but you were so enthralled by your dog that you didn't even know I was there." Then he said, "I promise now I won't, 'cos I've seen what that dog can do."'

But at eleven years old, Khan was ready to retire. Marjory had another dog earmarked for her and had just four days between Khan retiring and her new dog starting, but, she recalls, once you'd had a dog life becomes so much harder without one. 'It was terrible. I never went anywhere, I didn't actually do anything. I was scared to go out.'

The training a dog needs to go through to reach the level of reliability, steadiness and consistency required is intense, and not every dog succeeds. One of the hardest things required of them is to ignore most of their natural instincts while out on a walk: no sniffing of pavements or lamp posts, no reacting to other dogs they might meet or getting distracted by someone playing ball in the park.

'I always find it amazing that so many of them are able to do that,' said Penny, as together we walked along the street with one of her newer dogs. 'But often once they get further down the line, I think they develop an understanding that they have a responsibility for their handler, and actually they're so busy concentrating on the work that they do forget all that other stuff.'

Four weeks into her training and Folly, a fourteen-month German Shepherd/Retriever cross of tremendous beauty, was getting more confident about working in the harness and was learning what Penny called 'end behaviours'. We walked through the streets of the local town and never once did Penny's attention to the dog and what it was doing waver. I began to see what Penny saw – not a familiar street, a pavement, a pedestrian crossing, but instead a series of obstacles that have to be negotiated in the smoothest way possible. If there is a bin on one side of the pavement and another obstruction on the other, the dog needs to choose a path directly between them to make sure the handler won't bump into anything. If the pavement comes to an end at the turning of a road a dog must notice, stop and sit, whether a car is coming or not. At this stage in her training Folly required constant instruction from Penny and lots of praise – that positive reinforcement she'd told me about – when she did something right. By the end of the twenty-minute walk, both dog and Penny were exhausted from the extraordinary level of concentration both had had to employ, but Penny still had another dog to work.

'This is Cody,' she said, as a pale Golden Labrador jumped from the van and stood patiently as Penny fitted his harness. 'He's been in training for nearly fifteen weeks, so he's coming right towards the end of that training period. He's a really bright dog, very motivated by food – a proper Labrador, will do anything for a treat!'

A transition happened as soon as Penny put Cody's harness on. It was subtle, but obvious enough even for me to notice it. Cody appeared to shift from 'waggy, smiley Labrador' to 'dog-with-purpose'. And sure enough, as I walked alongside him and Penny I was aware that this was a dog who understood exactly what was required of him. As we negotiated our way around the town, Penny remained largely silent and gave him no hand cues.

'At this stage in his training, I'm expecting him to stop and sit at every kerb without any input from me. The same with obstacles. I would expect him to avoid obstacles by moving left or right as we approach them and to do the job as if I was in a blindfold.'

But there are times when these most obedient of dogs have to actively choose to disobey an instruction. If the handler is asking their dog to cross a road, the dog should only obey if there are no cars coming.

'How on earth do you train them to do that?' I asked Penny.

'We try and teach them that the car is a hazard and not to cross the road while a car's there. So I give him a forward signal with my hand, and at the same time I say wait.'

'Even I'm confused!' I laughed. 'Surely a dog is going to look at you like you've gone mad?'

Penny conceded that it did seem like a very mixed message but the dogs very quickly seem to pick up not to move forward when a car is there. Once the road is clear, they are then given the 'forward' signal and a vocal cue, followed by lots of praise.

'It's quite an unusual thing to expect the dog to actively disobey you some of the time and not others, but they are just very clever.'

And as if to prove it, Cody sat patiently at the kerb waiting for a car to go by.

We got back to the quieter part of town and Penny asked if I wanted to have a go. I took the metal handle that is attached to the harness at about the point of the dog's shoulder blades. As Cody moved off I became instantly aware that I was connected to him in a way that is entirely different from anything I've experienced before. None of my dogs go on leads very much because we are lucky enough to live in a place where they don't need to, but walking a dog on a lead doesn't give you any of the same physical awareness of a dog's gait that I got from the harness. Equally, when Teg walks beautifully to heel, almost brushing my leg, her eyes often raised to mine, we feel in step, almost like dance partners, but I don't actively feel her every step and movement. The only experience I could come up with that came close was riding a horse, when you are aware of every footfall, change of pace, and, if the horse is nervous about something, tensing of the muscles. But more surprising was the sensation that the dog was the one in control and in charge. I tried closing my eyes and was amazed at how easily I felt able to surrender to the will of the dog, how aware I was of every change in speed and posture, how protected I felt. And now I could begin to see why, when Khan came into Marjory's life, it had such a dramatic life-enhancing effect, and why when he retired and she was without a dog for a few days, she felt utterly unable to face the world.

Marjory's current canine companion is a large, shaggy Golden Retriever called Mouse. He is her fourth dog and quite possibly her last. Throughout our chat he lay beside her, apparently in a deep slumber, but every now and then he would twitch or raise his head just to reassure us he knew exactly what was going on.

'We gelled straightaway,' said Marjory. 'Absolutely straightaway. We did a walk, what they call the matching walk, where the instructor decides whether the dog is actually for you and it was amazing, 'cos the instructor said to me, "Have you walked this dog before?" I said, "No." He was just an amazing dog, seemed to know what I needed, what I wanted.'

I wondered whether, four dogs down the line, it wasn't just because she was a more experienced handler, but she shook her head. 'He just seemed to understand the way I worked, the way I spoke, it was an instant bond.'

Mouse is twelve years old and has been retired for a year but this time Marjory couldn't give him up. I asked her why and she started to say something but her voice caught in her throat. 'I'm going to get upset and I can't help it.' She took a breath. Mouse looked up at her. 'He was far too precious and far too loyal. I felt that he was just too good to me and he's seen me through lots of different things in my life and I couldn't do it. When I broke up with my long-term partner Mouse was very much a part of that. It was very traumatic for me and he just was there all the time. The tears would come and he would just put his head on my shoulder or my knee or cuddle in. There's been things like losing family members, family members dying and stuff like that, again, he was there. Job change, problems at work, things that didn't go well and he always seems to know when something's not quite right.'

So Marjory was faced with a stark choice. Mouse could be rehomed and she knew that he would be very happy and make someone a wonderful pet, but she would lose him. However, she knew he had come to the end of his working life and had to retire. If she kept him she wouldn't be able to have another dog and would have to rely on her despised cane. She chose to keep him. 'He's my pet!' she said with a smile. And Mouse lifted his head from the floor and gave her a look of unsurpassed adoration.

'But,' I asked, 'once the harness was off and replaced by a lead, did he understand that his job was done and his role had changed?'

'Absolutely, and I would never have believed it, but one night we were going up to the bus stop and there's these barriers that you go through. He was having a crafty sniff at the lamp post a thing he's never done and it was as if he was saying "You sort it out yourself". And I laughed and laughed and laughed and cuddled him and I cried and

I laughed and I was standing at the bus stop and I think people must have thought I was a bit mad, I couldn't stop laughing. He just knew that he didn't need to work any more.'

Chapter 12
Your Secret's Safe

Kush

The average dog is a nicer person than the average person.

Andy Rooney, American radio and television writer

I was hearing it again and again. Mouse had helped Marjory deal with difficult and traumatic events in her life, as well as being her guide. Joey made Lance Corporal Victoria Emberson feel less lonely; Oddy was Lance Corporal Slack's best friend. Tim Fogg and Matt Hammersley both eulogised about the feeling of being out with a team of dogs in which they had complete faith. Dogs may be able to perform all manner of tasks for us, from protecting us, finding us when we are lost and getting us to the most difficult and hostile places on earth, but perhaps the main reason the relationship between humans and dogs has endured for so many thousands of years is not simply because they are so adaptable, so eager to learn, but maybe because they trigger something in our brains that makes us feel good.

A young man called Dan was going through a tough time at home, and alcohol was his solace. One day after a particularly heavy drinking session he fell, knocking himself unconscious and ended up having emergency surgery to staunch the bleeding on his brain and fix his fractured skull. After seven weeks in hospital he was still unable to walk properly, his speech and memory were both affected and he went from being an outgoing, fun-loving person to a virtual recluse. His occupational therapist suggested to Dan's mum that he needed something that would give him a purpose again, a structure to his day. Scamp was able to provide exactly that. He wasn't a dog with any special training, in fact he had had no training at all. He was a three-month-old puppy that had been abandoned and taken in by the Dogs Trust. But Scamp was able to do something that no one in the medical profession could – he made Dan laugh again. He got him outside in the fresh air, helped him meet people and make new friends, gave him a sense of responsibility which in turn persuaded him to stop drinking.

'It's been a tough fight,' said Dan, 'and without Scamp I know I would have lost.'

If Florence Nightingale had heard Dan's story she would have wandered away down the corridor with her lamp, nodding knowingly. She had observed that small animals helped reduce anxiety in children and adults living in psychiatric institutions, and in her book *Notes on Nursing* she reported that being with animals helped patients recover. She wrote that book in the late 1800s. In the 1930s Sigmund Freud reported that his patients would feel less inhibited and more able to talk if his dog Jofi was in the room. In the 1960s Boris Levison, a child psychotherapist, presented a paper to a meeting of the American Psychological Association. In it he told the story of a nine-year-old patient who refused to speak. That changed when Levison brought his dog Jingles to the sessions. The paper was dismissed.

Even today, with all this evidence, both anecdotal and, increasingly, scientific, which tells us interaction with dogs and other animals is beneficial in all sorts of ways, there is a good deal of scepticism. Get Liz Ormerod on the subject and you won't get her to stop. But could that finally be about to change?

Liz told me, 'It's a very exciting time just now. We're on the cusp of something really big. People are beginning to take this seriously and the conference this year is going to be great. We've got people coming from all over the world.'

She paused, briefly, for breath. 'You should come!'

'When is it?' I asked.

'Saturday.'

'This Saturday?'

'Yes!'

It was Wednesday. 'Where is it?' I asked.

'Copenhagen.'

'I'll see what I can do.'

After a bit of a diary juggle and some frenetic Googling I found a flight and a hotel room and emailed Liz to say I'd be there. She had clearly been in no doubt that I would come. 'I've been in touch with the committee and they have invited you as this year's special guest. I've accepted on your behalf. See you there. Take a train from the airport. Taxis cost a fortune.'

My academic friends spend quite a lot of time going to conferences and I'd always wondered what went on. Were they an incredible meeting of fine minds, a battleground for brainy egos or simply an excuse to get away from home, drink too much and do something inappropriate with a professor from Idaho? My first impression, as I walked into the principal room of Copenhagen's conference centre, was that I had stumbled on a mildly highbrow coffee morning. Little groups of mainly women in casual clothing were sitting at tables or standing together holding mugs of coffee and munching on – what else? – Danish pastries. But no, this was the annual symposium of the International Association of Human Animal Interaction Organisations, or IAHAIO, which if you say it properly sounds like you are yodelling. The subject matter: 'Advancing Human–Animal Interaction beyond boundaries: Developing Our Road Map for the Future'. I was given a list of delegates which was as impressive as it was international. People had come from the States, Japan, Israel as well as from all over Scandinavia and Europe. I poured myself a coffee and headed for an empty chair next to a tall, friendly-looking man.

'Is this chair free?' I asked.

'Sure, come and join us. I'm Michael.'

Michael Kaufmann is the Farm and Institute Director at Green Chimneys Children's Service in Brewster New York. It is currently treating about two hundred children who have been classified or diagnosed with a mental-health disorder, from autism to anxiety and depression. Some are as young as five. On average they have been hospitalised psychiatrically twice and will take two or three different medications. They are, as Michael put it, 'children who are sort of psychiatrically in trouble'. Alongside more trad- itional methods of helping and supporting the children, animals play a very key role. Michael recounted some- thing that had happened just before he left for Copenhagen. It concerned a nine-year-old boy who had been at Green Chimneys for over a year. He came from a very disrupted, abusive family and Michael described him as a 'primal child' with a low IQ and very little ability to see other viewpoints.

One day the boy saw Michael feeding the goldfish in the pond outside his office. Michael asked him if he wanted to feed them and he agreed. From that day the boy would come and ask Michael if he could feed the fish. Michael told him he could, but he would be depending on him; if he didn't feed the fish they would go hungry. Michael gave a delighted giggle. 'He said, "Well, Mr Kaufmann, I'm going home for the weekend, I won't be here." I go, "OK, well, that's fine, aren't you excited?" And he looks at me and goes, "No, what I'm saying is who's gonna feed the fish? I'm not here." And that was a profound moment because it showed his ability now to think how his absence might impact another living being. And it was such a subtle thing, but that's how we see the progress. It's not about sky rockets going off, it's rarely that. The change happens over time as the children build relationships with animals, as they transition from being the ones that are taken care of to becoming the caretakers.'

Over the weekend I heard many such stories. Richard Griffioen, a Dutch PhD student, told me how his Down's syndrome son inspired him to have a complete career change when he saw how interaction with dolphins and the family dog helped his son learn to speak. Dr Andrea Beetz, a lecturer, researcher and psychologist, told me about a young patient of hers with selective mutism. The girl would only speak to her parents in whispers and wouldn't speak at all to anyone else. Andrea uses hypnosis as a form of therapy and the little girl's parents had brought her along to see if that would help their daughter. Andrea has a dog which she brings to her consultation room. He is not a therapy dog, but she has seen over the years that a dog's presence can be helpful. During that first session the little girl didn't speak, but showed real interest in the dog. When she arrived for her next session, Andrea told her that it was the dog's birthday. The little girl whispered to her mother to ask Andrea to leave the room so that she could say happy birthday to the dog. From that moment she started to whisper to the dog, as long as Andrea was talking to her mother and not listening to her. 'And before long,' recalled Andrea, 'without any hypnosis by the way, she was talking to the dog while I was still there.'

Dogs can have a similar effect on autistic children. Dr Marie-José Enders-Slegers is a clinical psychologist studying the human–animal bond. As part of her research she went to interview the mother of a three-year-old boy. During the two hours Marie-José was in the house the little boy stood in the kitchen pouring water in and out of a bowl. He didn't say anything or react in any way to Marie-José being there. His mother told her that he never spoke to anyone, that he had no friends and she couldn't take him out because he would just run away. His doctors had given up and advised that he be sent to an institution. But his mother had read about autism service dogs and, in a final bid to keep her son at home, applied for one. They were accepted and a Black Labrador came into their lives. It wasn't an instant success. The change took some getting used to for the little boy, but gradually he started to venture out with his mother and the dog, he became less depressed and started to talk. And there were also unexpected benefits for the mother, who had been largely isolated from her community by the demands of her son's condition. When she went out with the dog, her neighbours felt more able to approach her because the dog gave them an easy way to start a conversation. She started to have something of a social life.

One morning the dog was ill and couldn't get out of its bed. The little boy, who like so many people with autism never displayed any empathy, went straight to the dog, hugged it and rubbed its belly. Marie-José smiled. 'The mother told me, "I was crying. It was the first time I had seen my son have feelings for someone else." And now this little boy is so happy, he is in school, he has friends, it's great,' Marie-José told me. 'There are lovely films of these autistic guide dogs on the internet.' Indeed there are. Just don't watch them if you are wearing mascara. You'll end up looking like Alice Cooper.

But it was Brinda Jegatheesan's story that really stayed with me. Brinda was born in Singapore and worked as an English-language teacher in a school for the children of Japanese expatriates. There were three class levels – Class A for children who were more fluent in English, Class B for intermediates and she, as a Japanese speaker, taught Class C students who had recently arrived from Japan and students with disabilities such as autism, Down's syndrome and learning difficulties. One day a colleague knocked on her door and presented her with a nine-year-old boy. 'This is Tomo. He's been demoted.' Tomo was a Class A student, but his teacher said he was non-communicative, cried a lot, showed no interest in his academic work or working with his classmates, and preferred to sit by himself. He was failing. Brinda took him into her class and noticed that not only did he prefer to be on his own, but also seemed to be rather depressed. She talked to his mother, who told her that far from being mute, her son was trilingual. She was Chinese, the boy's father was Japanese and Tomo was fluent in Japanese, Mandarin and English. 'But,' said his mother, 'he doesn't seem to have many friends. We don't know what is going on. Can you perhaps tutor him after school?'

Brinda felt desperately sorry for the child and told his mother that although she didn't teach outside school hours, she could bring Tomo over to her house two afternoons a week. Brinda had two Golden Retrievers named Kush and Babe. Babe showed no interest in Tomo, but the other, Kush, rushed up to the little boy to greet him in the wonderfully over-enthusiastic, tongue-lolling, tail-wagging way that a Golden Retriever has. 'Tomo was terribly wary of Kush and would show signs of panic,' said Brinda. 'He didn't want to have anything to do with dogs. And so I had to hold Kush back and Tomo ran to the chair and pulled his legs up so they didn't touch the ground.' This went on for months. Every time Tomo arrived Kush would try and greet him, Tomo would stand still with fear and Kush, disappointed, would retreat to the sofa. But the breakthrough came when Tomo's mum forgot that Brinda had cancelled a session one weekend and dropped Tomo off as usual. Only Brinda's husband was home, so, unsure what to do with the child, he gave him some milk and cookies and said he could sit and watch the football with him. When Brinda returned home a couple of hours later she couldn't believe her eyes. Tomo was playing with Kush. 'I think Tomo was left to fend for himself because my husband was watching TV and Kush kept pawing Tomo for more cookies. My husband told me that he'd said, "Don't be afraid, just give him the cookie," and then continued to watch the football. It was when Tomo's healing began.'

Tomo would come rushing for his afternoon classes with Brinda, throw his school bag on the patio and spend time playing with Kush, teaching him Japanese words, and eventually he started to talk to Kush about what had been going on at school. Brinda's eyes filled with tears. 'I could hear him talk about bad things happening to him in school and so weeks later when I thought the time was right I probed Tomo, while he hung out with Kush, about his school life. Tomo talked about being bullied. His Japanese classmates did not want to play with him, that he was not allowed to sit with his Japanese friends to eat his lunch because he brought Chinese food at times, and his chopsticks were Chinese chopsticks. I didn't even know there was a difference and he said, "Yes, *sensei* [teacher], there is a difference. Chinese chopsticks are blunt at the end and Japanese chopsticks are fine at the end; the quality is different." So his mother, being Chinese, obviously gave him what his classmates considered the non-Japanese chopsticks and so he was ostracised for that and he spent his time eating lunch alone. I just thought, how could I, as a human being, as his teacher, not realise this is what has been going on? Instead it took an animal who doesn't speak English or Japanese, who has no professional teaching qualifications, to bring out something that we, as professionals, had failed to discover.'

Tomo and Kush became steadfast friends, Tomo's state of mind improved, as did his self-esteem and he started to enjoy learning again. He didn't feel so isolated at school because he had Kush to talk to. One day Brinda brought Kush into the school, because her home was being painted.

'Kush was an eighty-pound dog, a gorgeous, handsome-looking fellow. When I brought him into the classroom all the kids were completely mesmerised by him. But they were afraid too because he was so big. And then in walks Tomo, and what do you think happened? Kush goes straight to Tomo and Tomo hugs him and the kids were in complete shock. In that moment I saw Tomo's status change from this ostracised kid to the class hero. I didn't have to do anything after that. Within a year he was back in Class A.'

Not only did Tomo's life change, but Brinda's too. She left Singapore for the States and is now associate professor at the University of Washington in Seattle and Vice President of development for IAHAIO. Her area of study is the value of interaction with animals for vulnerable children.

But it is not just children who respond in these remarkable ways to animal interaction. People of all ages with a whole range of issues find that association with an animal makes a huge difference. There was much talk at the conference about the elderly. One of the single most stressful things for anyone going into a care home is not being able to take their animals with them, yet research shows that elderly people allowed to keep their pets are healthier, happier and require far less medical intervention. In the States, where the law does allow people to keep pets in sheltered housing, it has been discovered that it is not just the pet owners that benefit, but the whole community of residents.

It's a subject that makes Liz Ormerod's eyes flash with

fury. 'I simply don't understand why this law hasn't been passed in the UK. Every year 140,000 people in Britain have to give up their pets to go into sheltered accommodation or residential care and a third of those animals will end up being euthanised, which causes enormous distress to their owners. Yet people with pets require less GP visits – fifteen to twenty-one per cent less – and are far less likely to suffer a heart attack or stroke. A simple change in the law could save the health service so much money.'

'Is this your current battle, then?'

Liz nodded. 'I won't give up.' And I believe her, because Liz has been doing battle in one form or another for the last thirty years.

She trained as a veterinary surgeon, graduating from the University of Glasgow in 1975, and went to work at an inner-city charity clinic for people who couldn't afford private veterinary fees. She loved the work, because, she told me, 'It was such a challenge.' Many of the people she saw had very little idea of how to look after animals, but, she discovered, this was not wilful neglect. 'They were doing their best, but the best they knew,' said Liz. 'There is an old wives' tale that says putting sulphur or an onion in a dog's water bowl will protect it from distemper. There's another belief that keeping a dog on a lead is enough to stop it getting infected, or that a dog is immune to distemper until it is six months old.' So people didn't vaccinate their dogs. 'They would also think that if a dog had a cold, wet nose and it was still eating it was OK, but in the meantime the dog would have a lump that was growing and growing and sometimes it wouldn't be brought into the surgery until it was enormous – the size of a small suitcase.'

But many of the people Liz met over her time at the clinic were similarly ignorant of their own health needs. Their children wouldn't be vaccinated either. They wouldn't think to bother a doctor if they discovered they had a small lump if otherwise they felt OK. They knew very little about nutrition or preventative medicine or hygiene. As Liz put it, these were people who 'had fallen through the cracks'.

Over her time in Glasgow Liz developed what she thought of as her 'one health approach', helping her clients to learn as much about their own health and wellbeing as their pets. But she had also discovered something else that at the time, in the early 1980s, no one else in the UK seemed to have acknowledged. 'I'd recognised working with the Glasgow population that people were living in dire circumstances with high levels of social deprivation and poverty. My clients were mostly unemployed, elderly, infirm, disabled, or had mental-health issues. People had drug and alcohol addiction problems, or were living with people with drug and alcohol addiction problems, and often living with violence. But if they had a good bond with an animal, it was like a life jacket. Because of that bond they were resilient, they could cope.'

Liz's quest, when she moved south to Lancashire to run her own practice with her husband, was to educate other professionals in health and social care and education about this bond and how she thought that would apply to their work. 'I just thought, there's something very special here, I want to explore it.' But she was met with a great deal of resistance. She wrote to schools – and received not a single response. She wanted to introduce suitable pets into the residential care facilities and into sheltered accommodation. She approached her local council believing that if she explained the benefits her ideas would be taken up in a matter of weeks. Nothing happened. It was, she admitted, hugely upsetting and demoralising. So one day, when she had fifteen minutes to spare between house visits before she went back to the surgery and she was passing a school, she thought, 'I'm just going to speak to the headmaster! So I just went in, and said, I'm the local veterinary surgeon, I've just taken over the practice and I'd like to teach the children animal welfare. He said, what a good idea, when can you come?'

'Why did he change his mind?' I asked.

'He'd never got my letter,' Liz said. 'He thought his secretary probably hadn't thought it was worth him reading and put it in the bin.'

Those first lessons were a success and Liz soon found her way into most of the other kindergartens and junior schools in the district. The senior schools followed and then came a big breakthrough. The probation service asked her to work with youth classed as 'at risk', and the prison governor of a new high-security prison asked her to set up a programme for lifers. She started by introducing fish and birds into the prison and occasionally a visiting dog. The results were remarkable.

'People became happier, less stressed, more relaxed, more talkative. Relationships started developing between other residents and between residents and staff. The prison officers became much nicer to the prisoners and vice versa, because they could each show care for something like a budgerigar. The prisoner's thinking, he's not that bad, he brought in the millet spray. And the prison officer's thinking, gosh, he looks after that bird really well, he's not totally bad. And it was just . . .' Liz paused for a moment, trying to find the right words. 'It was like we'd sort of sprinkled something, you know, something magic. It worked with the children – all ages of children – and then it worked with the "at risk" youth, and then when it worked with the prisoners, the lifers and I was thinking, God, we really are on to something here.'

But she still felt out on a limb, or as she put it 'like I was on another planet'. All that changed when she was awarded a fellowship to the States. It was there she met fellow Brit Anne Conway, a dog welfare campaigner, and went with her to a conference in Boston being held by a group of academics on the subject of human–animal interactions. It was at that conference that she came across people with assistance dogs. It was an entirely new concept to her. 'I was able for the first time in my life to talk to people in wheelchairs without feeling awkward and not knowing what to say or do because I just was seeing them as dog owners.' She was invited to see how the dogs worked and went out around the town. 'The dogs would operate the buttons for lifts and crossings on roads and open doors and pick up dropped items. They were helping these people live independently.' Not only that, she learnt that many of them felt that having a dog had entirely changed their lives.

'They were entering into human relationships, some of them had got married, some of them were going back to college, some of them had got jobs . . .'

At the end of the conference Anne Conway turned to Liz and said, 'This is what we need to do. We need to start training assistance dogs for people in the UK.'

I asked her if she had any doubts, given all the resistance she'd met trying to introduce animals into schools and prisons. 'I wouldn't have taken it on, on my own. Anne was very open to new things. She was a highly intelligent woman and she just had vision. She coerced me to help and I did so willingly. It was just so exciting to see how dogs could be trained to make such a huge difference to people's lives.'

Chapter 13
Can I Help You?

Jon and Varick

The bond with a true dog is as lasting as the ties of this earth will ever be.

Konrad Lorenz, Austrian zoologist

Liz and Anne set up Canine Partners in 1990. With the help of an occupational therapist specialising in the field of disability and the patronage of Roger Jefcoate, who later received a CBE for his services to disabled people, they trained their first three dogs, Alex, Angus and Alfred. In the ensuing years nearly six hundred dogs have been paired with people with all manner of disabilities, from ME and MS to spina bifida and cerebral palsy. I went to a leafy corner of West Sussex to visit the headquarters and watch some of the dogs being put through their paces.

At the headquarters I met trainer Rebekah Kendrick, who was working with Moxie, a Labrador/Golden Retriever cross who despite only being halfway through his training delighted in showing me how good he was at picking up keys, opening doors and getting tins off a shelf. He could even open the door of a washing machine and retrieve the clothes inside. The training is intense and the dogs are asked to do difficult and potentially stressful tasks, like going to a train station and getting on a train, and they need to be able to work with people who have varying needs and ranges of mobility. Rebekah told me she had trained a dog for a soldier who had been shot in Afghanistan and was left paralysed from the neck down. He couldn't reward a dog by giving him a stroke or a pat. The only thing he could do was use his voice, but the dog was utterly devoted to him. 'The key is the emotional connection between the person and the dog,' said Rebekah. 'Not every dog works for every person. It is like any partnership. And our job as trainers is to build up an extraordinary level of trust with the dog, so that it feels completely comfortable and happy doing the tasks they are required to do.'

'But if you have spent months building up a relationship with a dog, how can it transfer that trust to someone else, someone it has never met before?'

'Before going home with their dog, everyone comes in for a two-week residential training course. At first who-ever has trained the dog will work with the new partner, but gradually the trainer will start to step back and the dog will learn to take instruction from their new owner. It happens remarkably quickly, usually within just four or five days.'

And the differences these dogs make to people's lives goes far beyond the practical, although having a dog that can tidy up, help make beds, collect things off supermarket shelves and load the washing machine is clearly fantastic. It got me wondering if it's possible to train Badger, Bella and Teg to cook supper and hoover up their own dog hair.

But it is the emotional and psychological support they give which, if anything, seems even more important. As Rebekah said, it is all about connection, about the bond, and with that comes companionship, a sense of fulfilment, a regaining of confidence, independence and freedom. In the magazine the charity sends out to supporters, there are many heart-warming stories from people who describe how the partnership with their dog has been transformative. Katy Evans has cerebral palsy and really struggled when she went to university. She didn't feel able to talk to fellow students and they felt the same about her. She lost con-fidence and became increasingly isolated and introverted. When she got Folly, she became not 'the girl in the wheelchair', but 'the girl with the amazing dog'. It turned her life around and she graduated with a first class degree.

For Jo Hill it was the lack of privacy and time to herself that she felt so acutely after her accident. She had been an active, upbeat mother of four when a car crash left her wheelchair-bound and in constant pain. She was utterly reliant on people to help her with everything around the house and with her young family. 'I had no privacy any more.' When her Black Labrador Derby joined the family, she didn't need people around her all the time and regained some of that precious space and time to herself. 'The difference he made to my life and that of my family is almost impossible to encapsulate into words. He has given me back some things that I thought had gone for ever and some things I did not even admit to myself that I'd lost.'

And sometimes a dog will do something that goes far beyond anything they've been trained to do. If it hadn't been for her Golden Retriever Edward, Wendy Hilling knows she would be dead. She suffers from a rare skin condition that causes her skin to tear and blister at the slightest knock. Her throat is severely restricted and can close at any time, leaving her unable to breathe. One day she was making a cheese sandwich for her husband. She is, she said emphatically, never allowed to eat cheese because it is too dangerous, 'but for some reason I put a piece in my mouth, just to suck it, but all of a sudden I swallowed and the cheese stuck fast. I couldn't breathe and all I could think was "I'm going to die."' Her husband, who was in the garage, was totally unaware of what was happening. Her dog managed to let himself out of the kitchen, out of the house and ran to the garage door and barked and barked until Wendy's husband heard him. He got to Wendy in time to save her life.

There was a residential course in progress while I was at Canine Partners. One of the participants was Jon Flint, a delightful man, with an open, smiling face and a sort of gentle dignity about him. We had talked on the phone the week before and the story he told me left me reeling.

Jon joined the Royal Marines in 1994 at the age of nineteen. He undertook what some have described as the longest, hardest military training course outside the Special Forces anywhere in the world. 'I loved it!' he said. 'When you pass out of your training, you're superman. You're sort of Olympic athlete level fitness.' During the thirteen years he served he did three tours, one in Northern Ireland, one in Iraq and his last one, in 2007, was in Afghanistan. 'It was the best tour I'd done and the worst tour for my family. It was just bonkers.' By this time he'd been married to Sarah for two years, but he'd been away from her and his two teenage stepchildren for half that time. But it wasn't just the stress he was putting his family under that made him decide to leave. He started to feel mortal. 'There was maybe half a dozen times when I thought, I'm not getting out of this, this is it, this is me getting my ticket punched. There was one time in particular where I'd got pinned down on a ridgeline by enemy fire and I thought, oh well, Sarah's going to be so cross. She's going to be so pissed with me if I get slotted [shot].'

It wasn't an easy transition to civilian life. He often woke up thinking he was under fire and taking cover. He didn't think he had Post-Traumatic Stress Disorder (PTSD), but he struggled with some of the things he'd seen and done. He also had to get over the death of his best friend Lee, who he'd done his military training with and 'was like a brother' to him. Lee was medically discharged from the Marines and emigrated to New Zealand, but he and Jon always kept in touch and Lee was the last person Jon spoke to apart from Sarah before he left for Afghanistan. 'He told me to "stay safe". He died from a brain haemorrhage while I was there.' Sarah had been trying to get hold of Jon for days. Lee was on life support and she wanted Jon to have the opportunity to say goodbye to him. 'I missed him by twenty minutes. I was obviously sort of devastated. The Sergeant Major gave me the option to go back to Bastion to deal with it and I said no, because he'd want me to stay out here and do my job, he wouldn't want me to wimp out and use him as an excuse. I had a job to do, I needed to do it. So I went round the back of the building, cried for about twenty seconds, picked myself up and cracked on.'

It is hardly surprising, then, that when he left the Marines he went into what he described as 'a flat spin'. He'd only ever wanted to be a soldier, he had no GCSEs. He thought his future would be stacking shelves in a supermarket. It took him a good few months to settle down and adjust but then he was offered a well-paid job as a security guard by an international bank in London. He didn't like it much, but it paid the bills. To keep himself fit, he joined a rugby club, but then he started to get a pain in his back. At first he thought it was just a pulled muscle, but instead of getting better, the pain got worse. He'd been promoted at the bank but was struggling to do the work because of the pain.

'Did you have any idea what might have caused it?' I asked.

'I had a bit of a tumble on an exercise in '96.'

'When you say a bit of a tumble I'm assuming that's not just a sort of tripping over a paving stone sort of tumble. Did you fall some huge distance or something?'

'I spanked in from about thirty feet.'

Jon was on an exercise on the Isle of Skye when he fell while abseiling off a cliff. 'Did you get yourself checked out when you got back?'

'I went to see one of the medics 'cos I went black from my kidneys to my backside and he said it was just bruising.'

So it was years later when Jon finally went to see a specialist and had an MRI scan. They found a problem, but not in his lower back as he had expected, but between his shoulder blades. 'I was told, "You need to have surgery now otherwise you're going to lose everything from the chest down."'

Jon had a stress fracture. 'Probably from Afghanistan, running around with kit on. To compensate for it my body was growing an extra bit of bone that was starting to compress my spinal cord.'

'So this was unrelated to the fall you had in 1996?'

'Yes'.

The surgery saved him from being paralysed, but it left him with other problems, many neurological. He found that his left leg wouldn't communicate with his brain properly and he fell a lot. Nor had the lower back pain gone away. More tests, more scans, and more surgery and they discovered that he had another fracture in his lower spine. He'd been running around with a broken back for fourteen years.

By 2011 Jon had gone from being supremely fit to having a body that just didn't work the way he was used to. He became increasingly isolated because he was scared to go out. As a young man with an athletic build and over six feet tall walking with a stick, people would assume he had just hurt his leg playing rugby or skiing. 'But,' he said, 'I have the balance of a drunken toddler. If someone knocked into me I'd fall over and be in bed for three or four days in absolute agony, completely out of it on painkillers.'

So he didn't go out at all unless Sarah was with him as his bodyguard – 'which is pretty funny, 'cos she's tiny.'

As you've probably gathered by now, Jon takes stoicism to a whole other level, but even he admitted that life in 2011 was crap. He was still trying to work a couple of days a week, but it was taking more and more out of him. What's more, he had to give up the spaniel Sarah had given him when he left the Marines.

'Did you grow up with dogs?' I asked him.

'No, I was terrified of them as a kid. But Sarah's got this "dog"' – he supplied the inverted commas – 'a little handbag dog called Ratty and her parents had a rescue dog called Smuggler who was lovely and stopped me being scared. But after all the surgery I couldn't keep my spaniel Oppo any longer because I just couldn't exercise him enough.'

But Sarah came up with an idea. They live just down the road from Canine Partners and she suggested they go there to see if there were any dogs that had failed the training that they could offer a home. Over a cup of tea Jon was told they didn't think that a failed dog was right for him. Instead they suggested he apply for a qualified assistance dog. Jon didn't know how to respond. Both he and Sarah believed that he would get better; they talked about all the things they'd do when he got his mobility back. They had been told by a couple of doctors that Jon's condition was for life, but they simply hadn't taken it on board. It took him months to even consider having the assessment – by his physiotherapist, GP and specialist – that would determine whether or not he would be a suitable candidate for a Canine Partner. 'I thought at least one of them might say no, you don't need one, but all three of them said, "Yes. Definitely."'

Canine Partners work very hard to find a good match. 'They introduced a dog over a day and then I had the chance to go away and think about its suitability before we agreed to "go firm" for the two-week partnership course. The first two dogs they paired me with were fantastic, but they just didn't quite meet my particular needs as one was scared of trains, and the other was quite small so it was difficult for me to reach down to her head collar.' But then, in December 2011, Jon met what he called his 'Goldilocks dog'. Varick was just right. He was a Flat-coated Retriever, or as Jon lovingly describes him, 'a tail with an idiot attached', and, like all Canine Partners, he transformed Jon's life. He was cheeky, incredibly nosy and an endless source of entertainment, but when he was required to work he took his job very seriously indeed. He picked things up. If Jon fell he would go and fetch the phone. Jon had been made redundant on medical grounds, but had enrolled at a university and Varick went too. Varick took a huge burden off Sarah because she knew Jon had someone looking out for him if she went out. But the biggest difference he made to Jon was that for the first time in years he was able to walk down the street holding his wife's hand. 'Sarah always walked behind me to protect me in case someone bumped into me, but no one's going to miss thirty kilos of big, black Flat-coated Retriever. I'd clip his lead on to my belt, hold my walking stick in one hand and then I could actually walk down the street holding hands with Sarah.'

Varick, Jon said, was a tool, there to do a job, to get him where he needs to be. 'But the problem is you fall in love with these tools. They become part of your life and they sort of get right inside your soul. That's a snag.'

On 11 March 2015 Jon phoned his GP. He was having some sort of strange heart palpitations and his GP told him to call an ambulance. He was taken to hospital for what he thought would be a few tests before being discharged. Both he and Sarah decided to leave Varick at home with her son – and Ratty – because Jon had to go to London the next day to see a specialist and it would be a long, taxing day for the dog. But Jon ended up being admitted and it wasn't until the very early hours of the next morning that Sarah got home. Varick was lying on his rug upstairs, paws crossed, looking for all the world as if he was asleep. But he was dead.

Sarah had no sleep. She returned to the hospital later that morning and, leaving her bag on Jon's bed, went to find a nurse to see if they could go somewhere private when Sarah broke the news. While she was away the phone rang in her bag and Jon answered it. It was the vet. 'And he didn't know that I didn't know . . .' Jon broke down. 'He told me Varick wasn't with me any more, that he'd gone. And then I just . . . you know, howled, and Sarah came running in and I dropped the phone . . . I'd lost my baby boy . . . I can't describe the loss, it's, I . . . I don't know, it's the worst sense of loss I've ever experienced in my life . . . But one day I'll be with him again and it'll be better next time 'cos I won't have my injuries any more so we'll be able to go out and play properly and I'll be able to run around with him.'

Varick was only four years old when he died. No one knows why, but the most likely reason is that he had a heart condition that hadn't been diagnosed.

It took Jon months to come to terms with what happened. Sarah told me that he said he couldn't conceive of having another dog. 'I could never do this again. I could never go through this pain.' They buried Varick with his basket, wearing his best Canine Partners jacket with its commando flashes and some of his favourite toys, and kept other reminders in their bedroom including his bowl which they couldn't bring themselves to wash. Jon's health suffered, he got behind on his work at university because he found he couldn't concentrate for more than a few minutes at a time.

As Bruce Fogle writes in his book *Dog*, 'The greater the

level of attachment we have to our dogs, the more intense the grief we feel when they die – and the suddenness of a dog's death and role the dog played in life can exacerbate it.' Bruce's own dog Macy died when she was just six years old. He had lost other dogs, but felt the loss of Macy particularly keenly, perhaps because she was young, perhaps because the two of them had spent many months on the road together retracing the route John Steinbeck took for his book *Travels with Charley*. Bruce wrote movingly about the rituals he needed to undertake to help him deal with his grief. He dug a hole under Macy's favourite shady spot in the garden and buried her along with the eleven tennis balls she had found in the park the previous month and brought proudly back to the car.

Jon took to writing too. He started a blog, a tribute to 'Mr V' as he called him, with the subtitle 'Living Without A Shadow'. 'Because that's what I'm missing; a small part of me that is hard to define, but nevertheless, something is missing.' In the blog he writes about Varick meeting the penguins at the London Aquarium and about when he and Varick were asked to take part in the Closing Ceremony of the London 2012 Paralympics. 'I'm convinced that Varick thought that night was the night he finally got the recognition he deserved; that it was a really well-organised "Varick Fussing Event" with 80,000 people all cheering as loud as they could for him . . .'

He also writes about life without Varick. A month after he died Jon wrote, 'I'm stuck . . . I miss talking to him, I miss his company and the love that he gave me. I miss the confidence that he gave me to do things.' And the fear of being in public spaces, which has returned since he lost Varick. 'I feel invisible again . . . Now I feel vulnerable, even if I've got someone with me. The big problem is I know what's missing. It's my confidence, it's my protector, it's my Varick and I don't know how to fix it.'

Not long before I met Jon he posted another blog. 'It's time to take stock and hopefully – to quote a beautifully phrased bit of Royal Marine slang – get all my shit in one sock.' Five months after Varick had died he realised that even though Varick was irreplaceable, it was time for a successor, not just for his sake, but the sake of his family. He needed to regain some of his independence and release some of the burden on Sarah.

Jon and I talked for so long my phone battery died and I had to call him back on the landline. When he told me that Varick had died he broke down in tears. He had been so matter-of-fact about his own injuries and the dramatic effect they had had on his life that this sudden emotional outburst completely floored me. I let him talk on uninterrupted so that I wouldn't give away the fact that he had reduced me to tears too. Finally, when we had both gathered ourselves, I asked what stage he was at now. 'Canine Partners think they've found me a dog. I'm going to stay there next week to start training with him to see if he's a good match.'

I told him Canine Partners had invited me down to their headquarters to see how the dogs were trained. 'Could I come and meet you and see how you are getting on, if you feel up to it?'

'I'll give you my number and you can just text me.'

Jon did text and I went to meet him in one of the training rooms. Beside Jon's wheelchair sat a black Labrador called Jester. They had been training together for four days. I had been told not to engage with Jester because at this early stage he needs to focus only on Jon. Everyone was acutely aware how challenging this week was for Jon, perhaps no one more than Jester himself, who kept his eyes on Jon throughout our conversation. Every now and then Jon's hand would stray unconsciously down to stroke Jester's head. The time came when Jon was called away to begin training again. I shook his hand and wished him luck.

Jon and Jester

'Come on, Jester,' he said, 'are you ready?'

And Jester rested his head on Jon's knee and looked up at him as if to say, 'I am. How about you?'

Chapter 14
Life Changers

Lucy

The world would be a nicer place if everyone had the ability to love as unconditionally as a dog.

M. K. Clinton, American author

It was an admin day. I'd done everything else that I felt took priority. I'd taken the dogs for a run, cleaned out the chickens, walked around the sheep, picked some tomatoes and collected the windfall apples. I had a cup of tea, put some washing on, had a shower, made another cup of tea.

Letters, bills and receipts sat in piles on the kitchen table. Emails glowered unanswered in my inbox. The sun was shining outside. 'Dammit,' I growled and reluctantly plonked myself down in front of my computer. It pinged at me. Another email, swiftly followed by another ping and a second email from the same sender. 'Apologies!' it read. 'I'm not sure why the image didn't attach . . . Take 2!'

I clicked on the attachment and smiled. It was a scan of a note handwritten on a piece of yellow lined paper. 'Dear Kate,' it read, 'thank you for paying us a visit . . .' and alongside the message and the multiple signatures were two pictures of a dog. She had the body of an English Bull Terrier with some Staffy thrown into the mix, and looked like a gangster's dog, solid and vaguely threatening. One photo was of her standing on top of her kennel looking bold and a little bit cheeky and the other one made me laugh out loud. She had been wrapped in a duvet, so that just her head poked out and there was a teddy bear at her side. Her expression seemed to say 'I know you don't think I'm adorable, but I can be . . .'

The name of the dog is Lucy. She is a rescue dog that has struggled to find a new home. But her appearance is deceptive. She is not vicious, but suffers from severe anxiety. She doesn't like traffic, is nervous of other dogs and new situations, and can become distressed when left alone. But I'd met a young man who was helping to change Lucy's fortunes, a man who, like Lucy, has not had the greatest start in life. He too had behaviour issues and didn't have a loving home. When I met him he was an inmate at H. M. Youth Offenders Institution (HMYOI) Polmont in

Scotland. He and the other young men whose signatures adorned my emailed note are all students enrolled on Britain's first prison-based dog-training rehabilitation programme. It is run by a small organisation called Paws for Progress based in Stirling, and I had contacted them to see if I could come and see what they did.

'We'll need to get permission from the Scottish Prison Service, which might take a little while, but we'll be in touch.'

After several weeks I got the go-ahead. I flew to Edinburgh, picked up a hire car and drove to the University of Stirling.

The founder of Paws for Progress is a young, energetic woman with a shiny ponytail and a stud through her tongue. Rebecca Leonardi's childhood had been dominated by dogs. 'I loved dogs, and used to have imaginary dogs until my parents finally caved in when I was about seven.' But Rebecca's parents didn't get a puppy; instead they rehomed two Border Collies that had been rescued from a farm. They had been so badly abused they were terrified of people, and Rebecca recalls sitting with her older sister on the floor of the utility room at home and waiting for the dogs to feel brave enough to approach them.

'I remember my bum going numb because of how long we used to sit there. We didn't know what we were doing, we just somehow wanted to let them know that we loved them, that we were going to be nice to them.'

Their persistence paid off and within two weeks the dogs started to bond with the sisters, although it was to take many more months for the dogs to be able to cope with new places and new situations without being terrified.

That formative experience stuck with Rebecca and when she left school she knew she wanted to work with animals. She spent some time in Australia, mainly working with horses, and when she returned to the UK in her mid-twenties she carried on working in animal care, although, 'I was mainly cleaning up poo!' she laughs. She credits the arrival of another Border Collie in her life for giving her the impetus to find out what other opportunities might be out there.

'Ellie was a very highly strung, quite neurotic, very anxious, very frustrated, and very confused young dog. She'd had five homes in the first eight months of her life and ended up first in Battersea Dogs Home and then at the Border Collie Trust.'

But, as Rebecca gradually discovered, with careful training Ellie grew in confidence and her true character came to the fore. The once nervous, worried little dog grew to be an extrovert. 'She wanted to be the centre of attention. She loved being with people and loved trying to figure them out.' It was Ellie that inspired Rebecca to enrol at the University of Stirling to study psychology, investigating particularly the relationship between humans and dogs.

'Where did that interest come from?' I wondered.

Rebecca didn't hesitate. 'It came from my own very positive experiences of training my own dogs, the enjoyment and fulfilment I got from that. I had learnt how rewarding it was to develop that partnership, develop ways of working together, learn to understand each other and to communicate effectively. I knew that felt fantastic when it worked.'

I understood completely. A couple of weeks before Teg had made me feel totally euphoric. I'd gone to meet Dewi Jenkins, a twenty-two-year-old farmer in Mid Wales. He has been training and trialling Welsh sheepdogs since he was just nine years old and has won the much coveted Ty Llwyd Bonnie Trophy three times. He also works with Border Collies and in 2015 won the One Man and His Dog Young Handlers Award. His dogs work with both sheep and cattle and he kindly agreed to allow me and Teg to come and see him put some of his dogs through their paces.

I stood with Dewi at the top of a field that sloped away from us, like a natural amphitheatre. At the bottom, perhaps five hundred metres away, were the cattle. The two dogs Dewi was working with were much smaller than Teg and I couldn't quite believe they could get a sizeable herd of Welsh Black cattle to do what they wanted. On his command the dogs didn't hesitate, but raced down the hill, skirting around the back of the cattle. Once they were behind them they started barking, driving them forward and working together to keep them in a tight group, driving them purposefully up the slope towards us.

'If we move back now and to the side, they'll drive them round to follow us.'

Sure enough, the dogs did exactly that, but what was really impressive was that the cattle at no point seemed harassed or panicked. They came quietly and calmly up the hill following the exact line the dogs wanted them to take.

'Have you tried your dog with cattle?' asked Dewi.

'I haven't. I'd love to and I think she would too, but I'm not sure we are quite at that stage yet and I would be very nervous about letting her loose on someone else's herd.'

'Well, let's see how she does with the rams, shall we? They can be quite intimidating so it'll be a good test for her.'

Dewi drove the cattle back out of the field and brought in his forty Welsh rams. They were incredibly handsome beasts, with fine sets of curled horns and in the peak of condition.

'Are you sure you're happy to let Teg loose with them?' Dewi nodded. 'She'll be OK.'

I was ridiculously nervous. Teg, who had been in the back of Dewi's truck while he'd been working the cattle, was beside herself with excitement at being given her turn. 'Don't just go rushing at them, Teg,' I said to her as we walked back to Dewi, 'this is a big test for us. I'll do my best, but I need your help too.'

I asked her to sit. The rams had moved way down to the bottom of the field. She had never done such a long outrun before. 'Away, Teg!' She raced down the slope but as she got near the rams she hesitated, looked back at me. 'Away!' I called and after a split second she ran on, behind the rams. They stood their ground and she barked. Dewi looked at me. 'That's good, really good.' Teg was now bringing the rams up the slope towards us, but one of the rams tried to break away. 'Get back, Teg!' and she doubled back and the ram thought the better of it and went back to the flock. Teg was working hard, running from left to right, keeping them together and keeping them moving. I could feel my mouth stretching into a huge, daft, uncontrollable grin. She drove the rams to within six feet of us.

'Stand!' and she stopped and stood behind them, a commanding presence that kept them all together.

'How old did you say she was?' asked Dewi.

'Just over two.'

'Well, that was very good, I mean, she worked like a fully trained dog.'

'It must be your influence. I did give her a pep talk and told her that in front of you she really had to behave!'

'Seriously, you've got a great dog there. With some more training she'll be . . . well, she's good.'

'Thanks, Dewi,' I said and thought I would burst with pride.

Rebecca had noticed that dogs could have a similarly positive effect on other people who weren't their owners or handlers but who were vulnerable either mentally, physically or both. When her beloved grandfather was suffering from severe dementia and was frequently very distressed and unhappy, she would take Ellie to see him. He wouldn't always remember Rebecca, but he always remembered Ellie and would be able to recall memories of dogs he had when he was younger. Seeing how Ellie had helped her grandfather, Rebecca registered her as a therapy dog and they became regular visitors at a local secure mental-health unit. It was, according to Rebecca, a pretty bleak, unhappy sort of place. The patients were suffering from a wide range of disorders and many were at their lowest ebb.

'And yet they absolutely loved Ellie's visits. Ellie would

go in and she would do tricks with some people; she would play with other people; sometimes she would just rest her head on someone's knee. She seemed to instinctively know who wanted to interact and who didn't. And people would be laughing, clapping their hands, people who didn't normally get out of their beds wanted to be a part of it. It was just remarkable what could happen through those kinds of interactions, and it made me realise just how skilled some dogs are at bringing that out in people, and what a powerful effect that can have.'

It seemed a logical next step to Rebecca that when she came to do her Masters she should investigate further the psychological boost that animals like dogs could give to people, particularly those who were vulnerable. She decided to concentrate her research on the effect that prison programmes involving dogs have on the inmates.

'There are all these amazing programmes in America and Canada, Australia and Italy and Spain, and I assumed they were really common here in the UK too, but when I started to look into to it I couldn't find any. It seemed there were none at all.'

'And how do they work?' I asked.

'There's two main models, the rescue-dog training model, where dogs who do not have a home and will also be at risk of being euthanised for that reason, go to facilities within prisons where they can be trained by prisoners. Through that training the dogs are able to develop more skills and have a better chance of finding a new home. And the assistance-dogs programme, which teaches prisoners to train dogs for the disabled.'

'I can see how that benefits the dogs,' I said, 'but what about the prisoners?'

'I think you'd better ask them that yourself,' said Rebecca.

HMYOI Polmont is just outside Falkirk. Clutching my photo ID, a notebook and a pen and leaving everything else in the car – 'You can't take in anything electrical' warned Rebecca – I walked into reception. I was expecting it all to be rather gloomy and austere and gothic, but the building was modern and bright and the person who checked my ID, took my photo and handed me my pass, waved Rebecca and me through the security scanner with a cheery smile. We were escorted down a maze of corridors and through a series of hefty doors by a prison officer. 'So tell me how you ended up working here,' I asked Rebecca, as we emerged from one building and followed a walkway to another.

'Well, as I told you yesterday, there were no prison-based dog-training programmes in the UK, which seemed mad to me. There was so much evidence from other countries that they worked, so I thought I would try and set one up.' She did a lot of searching online and the main authority on the subject, the name that cropped up time and time again, was Liz Ormerod.

'I met her,' I said. 'I bet she was delighted to hear that someone else was wanting to champion the benefits of human–animal interaction.'

'She was fantastic!' said Rebecca. 'So supportive. She even invited me to come and stay so I could ask her anything I wanted and she would tell me everything she knew.

I'd also been in touch with Gary Waddell who was then the head of offender learning and skills for the Scottish Prison Service. It turns out he had been interested in the potential of these kinds of programme for years but had never been approached by anybody interested in developing that area of work.'

With Liz's help, Rebecca drafted a proposal, which Gary took to Polmont. The idea was approved but on the condition that it had to be evaluated at PhD level. 'There was a lot of interest as my idea coincided with a growing acceptance and understanding of the benefits animals can bring to people in a variety of contexts. I got three offers for funding from different institutions.'

Rebecca submitted her PhD proposal in 2009. Over the following two years, she underwent more training, started talking to dog charities about possible collaborations and finished her Masters degree. She decided that the most suitable type of programme for Polmont would be the rescue-dog model and right from the start, when they first started delivering the programme in 2011, she was stunned by the results.

'I have always been amazed at how much you can rehabilitate dogs, but I'm also amazed at how much people change, even people who've been up against very, very difficult things. They still have such a lot that they can bring. There are so many dogs and so many young people who don't have a lot of people who believe in them. But dogs are very good at reinforcing a person's confidence and I suspected that if the young men were given the responsibility to work out how best to help the dogs, with our support and guidance of course, it would give them a real sense of pride and achievement. I was blown away immediately by how capable these young men proved to be.'

The vast majority of HMYOI Polmont's inmates have had what Rebecca described as a 'negative experience of education'. Most had left school by the age of fifteen and almost half of them had no qualifications whatsoever. Rebecca decided that for the course to be effective it had to be entirely practical. There seemed no point in asking the students to write anything down because it would bring back all those negative associations.

Our escorting officer unlocked a final door and we went inside. Around a table sat six young men in tracksuit bottoms and polo shirts. Most of them had brutally short haircuts and the sort of cocky demeanour that only exaggerated their vulnerability.

'This is Gary,' Rebecca said. The prison officer shook my hand and asked me to step into his office. 'If any one of them scares you, or threatens you, or offends you in any way, just come to me.'

'But Gary,' I said, as I looked back at them through the glass, 'they're just kids.'

'Aye, I know, but they'll be a bit different from the kids you're used to.'

As I stepped back out into the classroom Rebecca announced that the dogs had arrived. The dogs all come from local rescue centres and are brought in every day. Each course runs five days a week for ten weeks.

'It is a big commitment for the students,' Rebecca had

told me. 'They have to give up things like their gym, their recreation time. They give up ever having a lie-in between Monday and Friday because the dogs have to take priority. It is one of the most intense programmes in the whole prison, but it is also one of the best attended.'

I followed the young men out into a yard where agility equipment was set up and there were separate areas where the dogs could learn things like recall and walking to heel. The four dogs I met that day were coming to the end of their training and Rebecca told me they were unrecognisable from the way they were just two months before. One of them was Lucy, the star of my email. Her young trainer, Don, had worked miracles with her, Rebecca told me. While I was watching, a truck pulled up outside the gate near where Don was working. Knowing vehicles scared her, he bent down and scooped Lucy into his arms and carried her down away from the road as the truck went past. I could see him talking to her, reassuring her, and once the last rumble of the truck faded, he carried her back and continued his work. He was being mentored by another inmate, a young man called Max, who had already done the course and had trained one of Rebecca's rescue dogs, Mojo. Mojo is a part Patterdale and when he first arrived on the course at Polmont he was a very nervous young dog who was unsure how to behave. And yet he had spent most of the time I had been in Rebecca's office sitting on my lap, looking adorable and giving no signs of his traumatic background.

'That was Max's doing,' said Rebecca.

'Did it feel good,' I asked Max, 'when you could see Mojo starting to improve?'

'It was brilliant,' he said with a shy smile. I watched him later helping with another little dog called Gus. He was calm, quiet and endlessly patient and seemed to have a natural empathy with the dog that was a joy to watch. Gary came and stood beside me. His job, he explained, is to work exclusively for Paws for Progress within the prison. 'It's just great seeing what this programme has achieved,' he told me, as we stood and watched the young men doing obedience training with their dogs. 'I'm really proud to be part of it.'

The programme has changed and developed over the four years it has been running, thanks largely to suggestions from the students themselves. After the first course Rebecca thought it would be a good idea to ask former students to come back as mentors for the new ones.

'It became clear very early on that some sort of continuity between courses would be really helpful. Initially my idea was that students from the previous course might continue to work with their dogs if they hadn't been re-homed, and then one day a week help other students. But one of our first mentors told us that although he loved working with his dog, he felt he would be able to fulfil his role better if he had more sessions just purely helping people. We took his advice.'

And it was the students who came up with another way of helping the dogs that really surprised Rebecca. 'It was this.' She handed me a folder. It was filled with neatly written pages, drawings and photographs. It was like a combination of a CV and a really detailed school report.

'But I thought you said that because most of the young men here had had such bad experiences at school you wouldn't even try to get them to write things down.'

'I know,' Rebecca smiled. 'If you asked them if they wanted to do any sort of education, they'd say no, but they wanted to do this. They wanted people to know what the dogs can do, to promote them and for people to understand what the dogs like and what they don't like. And they were going away and spending their evenings and weekends writing these reports. The potential for this to be developed towards educational qualifications was clear.'

I started to read one of the reports Rebecca had handed me.

Suzie is a lovely Staffy-cross with a big black patch over the left side of her face. She dislikes being overcrowded by strangers and being pushed to do something she doesn't want to do or is unsure of, but neither do I, so I can't blame her. She is the type of dog who, if shown the right blend of love, patience and attention, will, in return, go on to love you and become one of the most reliable friends you could have.

I could feel tears prickling the backs of my eyes.

'I know,' said Rebecca, 'it has that effect, doesn't it? And the young man who wrote all of this had come from quite a difficult situation. He'd been his mother's sole carer. His mother was quite severely disabled, and he had been trying to cope with that at the same time as being in a family who were quite consistently involved in the criminal justice system. He'd never known anything outside of that world of crime and hardship, basically.'

'Is he still here?'

'No, he went on to an adult prison following Polmont, but he's due for release soon. I saw him recently because I was running a focus group at his establishment. He spent his whole time wanting to tell everybody about what a positive experience he'd had at Paws for Progress, and what he'd been able to achieve. He was really pushing for it to be introduced into adult prisons as well.'

All the young men I spoke to were similarly enthusiastic.

'It makes us feel better.'

'It relieves stress.'

'Makes you more disciplined.'

But what about long term? Once the course was over, did changes in behaviour last? Was there an outlet for those newly learnt skills? As required by the prison service, Rebecca has been evaluating the programme since it began and I looked at the statistics. They were undeniably impressive. They show that all the students who had undertaken the course had gained qualifications as a result, many of them in core skills like communication and numeracy. Students finished the course feeling more motivated, better able to control their emotions, and with a greater understanding of the importance of giving something back. One of my favourite quotes from Rebecca's initial report is this one: 'When you first get your dog, it doesn't know nothing, then when you work with it you can see progress . . . It's not easy but it's good. It's good to see you're helping a dog that's come from nothing. I've never done nothing to help anybody in my life, so when I do this it makes me feel alright 'cos I'm doing something good.'

But there were two key areas that really leapt out at me. The first was the statistics comparing the number of disciplinary reports an inmate had received before he did the course with the number he received afterwards. There are three categories of offence – 'disobedience', 'vandalism', and 'violent and threatening'. There was significant reduction in all of them, but most markedly in 'violent and threatening' behaviour. Rebecca told me that the young men would resist getting into a fight because they knew that if they had to go to the orderly room, or worse, what they call 'the Digger', which is solitary confinement, not only would they miss out on the training, but their dog wouldn't be brought in from the kennels. 'They know how much the dogs love coming from the kennels, how excited they are when they get to us. For the students to know that a dog would be left behind in its kennel, sitting there, not getting to come in because of something they'd done, is devastating, and it had a massive impact on their behaviour.'

As one student put it, 'I think seeing how easily my dog changed his behaviour had a huge positive impact on helping me change mine.'

The second thing that struck me was how many people managed to find employment as a direct result of having done the course. George was a tall, quietly spoken young man who had been both student and mentor and was due for release just a couple of weeks after I met him. 'Do you know what you are going to do when you get out?' I asked.

'I'm hoping to get some volunteer work at the zoo,' he said.

Half the young men who take the Paws for Progress course have never had any kind of work experience. Combine that with few, if any, qualifications, a history of substance abuse (which is true for 93 per cent of them) and a criminal record, and their chances of finding employment are pretty negligible. But they become much more employable once they have completed the course, and Rebecca and her colleagues continue to support them after they are released, helping them find volunteer work that might lead to a permanent position. One got voluntary work at a boarding kennels and is now employed as the manager. Many go to work at rescue centres where their training skills continue to be invaluable. Some have ended up in conservation or forestry. A year after release, the statistics told me, 82 per cent of former students were living in the community and most of them were 'engaged in productive activity' such as education, training or employment.

And the dogs? One hundred and sixty-seven have been trained by the young men at Polmont since Paws for Progress began, and one hundred and sixty-one of them now live in new homes. And Don is hoping Lucy will be next. That morning she had passed her good-behaviour test, demonstrating that she could walk nicely on a lead, sit, lie down and come back on command and be able to be around other dogs and new people. She could now be offered for rehoming.

I went to congratulate Don. 'You must be really pleased

that all your work has given her the chance to get a new home,' I said.

'I am,' he said, as he sat with Lucy in her kennel, stroking her head and giving her treats. 'But it would be even better if she went to a foster home. Then when I get out she could come and live with me. We could look after each other, then.'

Chapter 15
Hide And Seek

Aran and Ned

If a dog will not come to you after having looked in your face, you should go home and examine your conscience.

Woodrow Wilson, President of the
United States 1913–1921

Researchers at the University of Miami discovered that when stories about dogs appeared in the *New York Times* they were almost three times more likely to be picked up by other newspapers the next day than non-dog-related stories. 'Thus,' the researchers wrote, 'we conclude that dogs are an important factor in news decisions.'

It is true that newspaper editors understand – and take full advantage of – the appeal of a good dog story, but, according to Matthew Baum, a professor of global communications at Harvard University, including a dog in a story can actually help bring to light issues that might otherwise get overlooked. A good example of this appeared in newspapers all over the world in the autumn of 2015: 'Meet Killer, South Africa's Most Successful Poacher-Catching Dog who Travels By Helicopter & Tracks Hunters for Miles. And He Bites'. It's not exactly a pithy headline but you want to read on. The story reported that a Belgian Malinois, born and bred in South Africa, had caught fifteen poachers in Kruger National Park in less than a year. The story of Killer's success highlighted the sad fact that even in this day and age, when science refutes all claims that rhino horn is a magic cure for cancer, impotence and all manner of other ailments, rhinos are still being killed. Rhino horn is made of keratin. It is basically the same stuff as our fingernails, except that our fingernail clippings won't fetch upwards of $60,000 per pound. Rhino horn is almost a hundred times more expensive than it was a decade ago – more valuable than gold, diamonds and cocaine – and ludicrously, people still want to buy it. And because it has such a high value, it is worth taking risks for. In 2015 over a thousand rhino were killed for their horns in South Africa alone. The poachers are well funded and well armed, usually coming over the border from Mozambique. Despite the likelihood of a seventy-year jail sentence if they are caught, they are not deterred, and park rangers are regularly killed if they are unfortunate enough to cross them. The problem has become so acute that many conservationists believe that at the current rate of poaching, rhinos will be extinct in the next twenty years. The success of Killer has encouraged the authorities at Kruger National Park to increase their army of dogs in the hope that with a higher risk of being caught, the poachers will stay away.

Dogs are being used all over Africa in an effort to combat poaching, and recently the David Shepherd Wildlife Foundation funded dogs and handlers to start patrolling the national parks in the Indian state of Assam, where not only rhinos but also tigers are at risk. But not all poachers are armed with automatic weapons and looking to make their fortunes. Some are simply local villagers trying to catch food for the pot or bush meat to sell. They may not have such sophisticated weapons, but their methods are every bit as deadly and destructive. Wire snares are simple, cheap, and effective. They also work indiscriminately, catching or maiming any animals unfortunate enough to stumble on one. While I was working in the South Luangwa National Park in Zambia, I saw all too frequently the damage snares do. One young elephant had a drastically shortened trunk thanks to a snare, a hyena – still alive – had one embedded in its neck. Our guides told us grisly tales of finding wild dogs, lions and cheetahs severely maimed by snares.

While I was there I also heard about the work of Megan Parker, an American biologist based in Montana. She spent several years based in southern Africa collecting data for her PhD on African wild dogs. These beautiful animals – sometimes called Painted Dogs because of their markings – are an endangered species, and they can be fiendishly hard to find, even if you know there is a local population. Their territories are huge, they can cover enormous distances in short periods of time, they are more active during the night than they are during the day, and they are brilliantly camouflaged, making the work of someone trying to study them and assess the size and health of a population frustrating, time-consuming and expensive. Megan and her team spent tens of thousands of dollars on flights in bush planes to try and pinpoint where the dogs might be. Once they found them, they would go in on the ground and try and dart some of the members of the pack to fit them with radio collars to make tracking them easier, but this had limited success.

Megan had always had an interest in dogs. She had spent much of her childhood training domestic dogs and had been a member of her local Search and Rescue team. Given that dogs have been used since the 1960s for detection work, Megan reasoned there was nothing to say that an animal capable of finding a lost person, or an illegal substance in a suitcase, couldn't be used to help her and her colleagues in the field. She knew that if they could train dogs to find wild dog scat – a slightly more scientific word for poo – they would be able to gather a huge amount of invaluable information in less time, at a fraction of the cost and in a way that was less bothersome to the wild dogs. You can learn a lot from poo. It gives you a good indication of density of population, what an animal is eating, whether it has any diseases. You can even extract hormones and DNA from it. The idea, eccentric as it might seem, worked, and it worked so well that Megan founded Working Dogs for Conservation. Her idea was to have a number of dogs that could be trained for specific conservation projects, and it wasn't long before she was asked back to Africa with her dogs to help on a cheetah-monitoring programme.

Megan was based in Zambia at the South Luangwa National Park and it was there that she, like me, became aware of the impact of snares. To work, snares have to be carefully hidden, making them very difficult for human beings to find. Could dogs do any better? 'Sceptics said that dogs couldn't detect metal, but no one told Wicket and Pepin that!'

Pepin, a Belgian Malinois, was working on the cheetah-monitoring programme and had proved to have 'almost magical' scenting skills. He took off after a scent one day that eventually led his handler to some cheetah scat. It was over half a kilometre away. And up a tree. Megan's other dog, Wicket, came from a rescue home. A big, black Labrador cross, she was, according to a woman who worked there, 'crazy'. She barked all the time, threw herself against the walls of her kennel and, as a result, no one was willing to give her a home, until six months later she was discovered by one of the Working Dogs for Conservation team. Wicket, it transpired, just needed a job, and would do anything as long as she was rewarded with a ball. Both she and Pepin defied the sceptics and had no problem at all finding snares.

A dog's nose is an extraordinary thing. No scientist, inventor, engineer or techy whiz-kid has come close to coming up with a man-made machine that can do the job as quickly, efficiently and accurately. An average dog has around 250 million scent receptors. Dachshunds don't have so many – around 125 million. Bloodhounds have 300 million. We humans have just five million and we dedicate only 5 per cent of our brains to analysing smells. Dogs use 33 per cent of theirs. When you've just made multiple cups of tea and can't remember which ones have got sugar in, you will probably be able to smell it, if you take a good sniff and concentrate. In comparison, as canine cognition expert Alexandra Horowitz describes in her book *Inside of a Dog*, a dog's nose is sensitive enough to 'detect a teaspoon of sugar diluted in a million gallons of water: two Olympic-sized pools full'. Combine a dog's nose with its willingness to please and you have an un-beatable tool that is as adaptable as it is accurate. Megan's dog Wicket has now been trained to detect an incredible twenty-six different scents, from Hawaiian Rosy Wolf Snails to the scat of Chinese Moon Bears. Pepin was one of the first dogs to be able to detect an invasive species of fish as it swum up a river. Dogs have been trained to find snakes, plants crucial to the lifecycle of one particular species of butterfly, and even to detect the presence of the larvae responsible for killing millions of ash trees in the United States. As Megan said, 'We really haven't asked a question that dogs haven't been able to answer.'

Megan's work has proved inspirational the world over, not least to Louise Wilson. After university, Louise worked as a volunteer for a company called Wagtail that trained detection dogs. A few months later the company offered her a job as a kennel assistant. She proved to be an excellent trainer and handler, and over time worked her way up to become the company's head of training. She heard about Megan's work in Africa and went out to work alongside her and to learn how she could apply the training Megan was doing with her dogs to aid conservation efforts in the UK. On her return she set up an offshoot of Wagtail, training dogs to find, among other things, great crested newts.

'This I have to see!' I thought. I phoned Wagtail's office and spoke to Aran, one of the trainers working both with detection and conservation dogs. 'Would it be asking you to give away all your trade secrets if I were to come and see how you work?'

'Not at all!' he laughed. 'We'd be happy to show you around. We're based in North Wales on a beautiful estate. It can be a bit hard to find and the phone signal's rubbish, but I'll send you directions and we'll see you at about ten o'clock on Wednesday.'

I climbed out of my car, feeling a bit like a new servant in an episode of *Downton Abbey*. Aran's directions had brought me to what had once been the very grand stable yard of the even grander house just visible over the rooftops. I pushed my way through a hefty wooden door, climbed a staircase, the stone steps worn smooth by centuries of feet, and found my way to the office.

'Shall we start with a cup of tea and a bit of a lowdown on what we do?' suggested Aran, and I joined him and his colleague Mike in the kitchen.

Wagtail was set up in 2003 by Collin Singer who had been a dog handler with the RAF for twenty-four years. One of the first contracts they were awarded was with the Border Force to find illegal immigrants on the northern French borders. No one then could have predicted what was to happen in the coming years, but even before the migrant crisis of 2015, Collin's dogs were finding huge numbers of people a year trying to get from France to Britain in ways I could never have imagined.

'Do you really need dogs if you are just opening up the backs of lorries to find people?' I asked – naively, as it turned out.

'You can't open up every single vehicle,' Aran explained. 'For every sailing there could be up to five hundred bits of freight that go on a ferry and they want the vehicles on that ferry as quick as possible, so not every vehicle can be opened or scanned. Not every vehicle is going to have a CO_2 probe put in or a heartbeat monitor on. And those don't always show up anything anyway. But dogs will take literally seconds to go around a vehicle. They can do five hundred vehicles easily and much more quickly than anything else.'

'But don't they have to go inside the vehicles?'

'No, they just sniff the edge of the vehicle, the corners of the freight container, the cab, the cab doors, and with refrigerated vehicles there might be drainage holes or weaker points in the structure where they sniff.'

'But a vehicle is going to be covered in human scents. How can a dog possibly differentiate between the scent of the driver, the people who loaded the freight, and someone who is there illegally in a matter of seconds?'

Aran smiled. 'Because they're incredible. It's very hard to even pinpoint what exactly the dog is detecting. Is it sweat, is it the smell of the clothes, is it the CO_2 that the people are breathing out? And the dogs there have worked out, for example, that there is always a driver in the cab, so they won't indicate on that, but if there are illegal immigrants hiding in the cab, they will. The most incredible find was in a sealed airtight tanker carrying something like gluten powder. A dog indicated on it and they pulled out a bunch of people, covered in white powder, who would definitely have suffocated if they hadn't been found.'

Most of the work the dogs do within the UK is searching for illicit tobacco and cash. 'We search a lot of shipping containers and self-storage units, where people store furniture and stuff like that. We might find three or four hundred thousand cigarettes that have either been smuggled into the country without paying any duty or that are counterfeit. We found seven tonnes of loose counterfeit tobacco in a sealed watertight container once.'

But finding tobacco in containers is one thing, finding illegal tobacco in shops that sell legal cigarettes is quite another.

'The dogs have been trained to ignore a legitimate cigarette gantry, but sometimes they'll indicate on it and you'll find counterfeit cigarettes hidden underneath. There was a time when a dog indicated on a tiled floor and it turned out the owner of the shop had built a pneumatic lift into the floor. He had a key fob in his pocket and when he pressed it the lift popped out of the floor and it was full of cigarettes.'

Mike showed me some pictures. 'They'll quite often hide them around ceiling lights or in walls. They'll use coffee, washing powder, chilli powder's a favourite, to try and throw the dogs off the scent, but it doesn't work. This is one of my favourite finds.' And he showed me a photograph of a tiled wall in a shower with a sort of drawer sticking out of it full of cigarettes. 'My dog indicated on the wall, and we found a switch in the stockroom and when we pressed it, this drawer came popping out!'

'The best one for me was not long after I qualified,' said Aran. 'I went upstairs to the flat above a shop and there was this big walk-in cage with two African grey parrots in it. The dog indicated on the cage and underneath the litter tray was a stash of counterfeit tobacco!'

'Would it be possible to see how some of your dogs work?'

'Yeah, no problem. We'll go over to the kennels and get Phoebe and Lucky to show you what they can do and then we'll take you out with some of our conservation dogs.'

While Mike went to get the dogs I followed Aran to one of the old stable buildings where a series of rooms had been dressed to resemble an untidy living room, with chairs, clothes and shelves of books, a desk with an old computer and printer on it and a radio playing. The adjoining room was more like an attic with piles of boxes and junk. Aran took a small plastic bag out of his pocket. In it was another plastic bag and in that was a gram of cocaine. He tucked it behind the plastic cover of the electricity meter so it was completely out of sight and quite high up. Mike came in with Phoebe, a two-year-old black Labrador, who was also an unwanted rescue dog.

'She's fantastic,' said Aran, as he put her harness on. 'Really responsive, great nose, great indication, everything you want. Her harness is like her uniform. Once she has her harness on she knows she's working.'

Aran had closed the door to the room where he had hidden the cocaine, just in case she found it too quickly. Phoebe started in the other room with what Aran called a 'free search', where she worked on her own. I imagined she might work quite slowly and methodically, but she worked hugely quickly, dashing around the room apparently randomly, tail wagging all the time. She passed the printer. 'We hid some drugs in there a few days ago on a training session,' said Aran. 'She's not giving a full indication but she knows that drugs were there once.'

'Really?' I had been watching her constantly, but hadn't noticed anything that gave me the impression she'd given any more attention to the printer than anything else in the room. 'What did she do that tells you that?'

'If you work with a dog regularly you pick up on changes. She did what is called a "check step". When a dog is searching and running or walking at a fast pace, it will suddenly stop and sort of skid and work its way back. They do that when they think they've picked up a scent they recognise.'

'It's pretty subtle,' I said. 'I can't even pretend I saw it!'

'It's practice, and knowing your dog. What she hasn't done yet is search anywhere high, she hasn't climbed up on anything or stood up on her back legs. That's something I will encourage her to do when we begin the systematic search.'

For this he sent Phoebe around the room again, but this time Aran used hand signals and commands, getting her to jump up on to shelves and windowsills and get into tight spaces behind furniture. He talked to her all the time, giving her lots of praise and encouragement.

'How do they find something that is way out of their reach? Even if she stands on her back legs she's not going to be able to get her nose very close to where you've hidden the drugs.'

'Scent falls,' explained Aran, 'and creates what is called a "scent pool" which spreads out. That's why a dog can find things even when they are tucked behind a beam in the ceiling or something like that. Let's go into the other room now and see how she does.'

Phoebe began her search. I held my breath as she passed beneath the meter where Aran had hidden the bag of drugs. She didn't appear to pause, but a few seconds later she was back, looking at the meter intently, standing rigid and still. 'And that's the full indication that tells me she's got it!' said Aran. 'Good girl, Phoebe!' and he threw her a tennis ball. She bounded joyfully after it, mission accomplished.

Mike brought in the second dog, Lucky, a young golden Labrador who was three weeks into his training in drug detection. In that short time he had already learnt how to recognise herbal cannabis, cannabis resin and cocaine, but had, until today, been working with relatively large quantities of cocaine. It was his first test to see if he could detect just a gram of it. Aran explained that although the way Phoebe worked had appeared rather random to me, she has a pattern, a method of working that ensures she has searched a whole room. Because Lucky is still learning, Aran and Mike let him do his own thing so that he can find his own most successful way of completing his task. 'He's a really clever dog,' said Aran, 'with a fantastic nose and he's nice and tall, which can help.'

I watched Lucky search the room. He wasn't quite as quick as Phoebe, didn't move quite so frenetically and seemed less confident. 'It comes with training and with practice. At the moment he is still learning the scents and developing his technique. And I'm being a bit mean to him because it is a big leap for him to find one gram of cocaine when up until now he's been finding four, but it helps us gauge what stage he's at. Oh look! Did you see him pick up on it then?'

Even I couldn't fail to miss Lucky's indication. He span around and jumped up against the wall, nose pointing up towards the meter. Aran threw the ball.

'And he's learnt that in just three weeks?' I asked, astounded.

Aran nodded. 'I told you. Dogs are incredible.'

'But are they really incredible enough to find great crested newts? Can they really be trained to do that?'

'Come on,' said Aran, 'we'll go out into the grounds and I'll show you.'

When Wagtail trainer Louise Wilson returned from her fact-finding mission in Africa full of ideas about how

Wagtail's dogs could be used for conservation, there was disappointingly little interest from potential clients. Eventually they were approached by Exeter University. The university was doing studies on the impact of wind farms on bat populations and wanted to know if a dog could be trained to detect bat carcasses. Pine martens were Wagtail's next challenge. Pine martens are found principally in Scotland, with small, isolated communities in England, Wales and Ireland. Members of the same family as weasels and stoats, they are incredibly rarely seen, unless you go to a certain cafe on the edge of the Cairngorms, where the local pine marten population has developed a taste for jam sandwiches. An academic was doing a PhD on pine marten populations and asked if Wagtail could help. Louise trained her dog, Luna, to detect pine marten scat to help establish the extent of the pine marten population in Ireland. It was the success of that study that proved the catalyst; interest in using dogs for conservation projects in the UK started to grow.

Training dogs to find newts is Wagtail's most recent project and has proved the most challenging. Newts, as Aran has discovered, don't have much of a smell, certainly not compared to a dead bat or pine marten poo. And they tend to hide away, under logs and stones in swampy areas at the edge of ponds. Great crested newts are a protected species, and building on sites where they are found will either be restricted or forbidden. Bucket traps are commonly used to establish whether newts are present, but they have to be left for several days. If dogs can be successfully trained to detect newts, they will be able to do it much faster. Britain's first and only newt-detection dog-in-training is Ned. He's an English Springer Spaniel who had all the right traits to be a great sniffer dog, except that he was a bit nervous around people. But for conservation work he is fine, because usually it will be just him and Aran out in the fields walking up and down in methodical lines, making sure they miss nothing. It was instantly apparent that this little dog loved his job. As soon as Aran got him out of the van and put him on his long lead he was off. We walked down a track through a wood and Ned was into everything, nose down, tail going like the clappers, racing between trees and patches of bramble, down into ditches with an almost manic determination.

'So do you know there are newts in this area?' I asked.

'No, but we have stunt newts.'

'You do?!'

'We have a special licence to keep and handle three great crested newts for training purposes. We can't use dead ones because obviously the scent will be different from live ones and it is live ones we need to find. While we're walking down here, my colleague Lauren is hiding a newt for us under a bit of bark. The problem is they don't tend to stay still, so she has to keep a really close eye on it in case it does a runner!'

We were coming to a fork in the track and I could see Lauren standing beside a tree looking intently at a piece of bark on the ground. Ned was still working his way down the verge, and then crossed over to sniff around the tree.

'Oh!' said Aran. 'Did you see him change then? He got a whiff of it. Watch him. He's trying to figure out where the scent is coming from. Good lad, Ned. Fetch on, bud.'

Ned was moving cautiously around the piece of bark and then he gave an indication, but seemed to be pointing behind it. Aran lifted the bark. There was no sign of the newt. 'That's where I put it,' confirmed Lauren.

'Careful, Ned, careful, where is it?' Aran was now on his hands and knees working right alongside Ned.

'Got it!' he cried. 'It had burrowed right into this long grass. Well done, Ned!' And Ned got to play with his beloved tennis ball.

'You can see how difficult it is, can't you?'

I nodded.

'But that's what's great about it. It's really interesting what the dogs pick up on and what they don't, it's all part of the training and we learn something new every single time.'

I wondered if there were any other species the dogs might be trained to find. 'We've had enquiries about training dogs to find Natterjack toads and smooth snakes. We've also got dogs out in Gabon working with a local company to try and find products of animal origin – things like ivory, cheetah skins, pangolin scales. We trained up local handlers. They love the dogs and love the work. There's an amazing video on YouTube of one of our dogs Lumi. They had set up a roadblock and a vehicle stopped and Lumi, who was still in training, indicated on it. They found a big holdall inside which they started to search. It was full of bush meat, but all of it legal – monkeys, porcupines and antelope – but then right at the bottom, underneath all this other stuff, was a giant pangolin, and that's illegal and that's what Lumi indicated on.'

But Aran told me that their strangest request came from a pest-control company. 'They asked if we could train a mouse detection dog. The thinking was that if a dog could find out where mice were coming in and out of a building, they could just block up the holes. There would be no need to use traps or bait.'

'And did you?'

'It had never been done before, but yes. We didn't train them using mice, but just the grease on a mouse's fur.'

'And it worked?'

'Of course it did. There seems to be nothing these dogs can't do.'

Chapter 16
Trust Me, I'm A Detection Dog

Doctor Claire Guest and Daisy

Dogs never bite me. Just humans.

Marilyn Monroe, American actress

Training dogs to find drugs, tobacco and even newts doesn't seem that far-fetched when you discover just how sensitive a dog's nose is, but in recent years it has come to light that dogs can do something that appears, on the face of it, to be impossible, indeed nothing short of miraculous. They can detect things that are completely invisible and, to human beings at least, have no smell at all.

A few years ago I was on a book tour, a forty-date journey that took me to bookshops, village halls, theatres and literary festivals all over the country. Very nerve-wracking it was too, because there was no guarantee anyone else apart from me would turn up to these events. I feared throughout that I would arrive to an echoing hall, with rows of empty plastic chairs and a pile of unwanted books on a trestle table. One of the venues I was invited to was the Mainstreet Trading Company, a book-shop in the Scottish Borders village of St Boswells. It was an evening I will never forget – for all the right reasons. St Boswells is what I consider a proper village. Its buildings are handsome rather than twee, there's a post office, a hotel, fish and chips and a green that plays host to the annual fair. The bookshop is on the main street that gives it its name and was once an old-fashioned department store. Now it is a sun-filled, bright room that pays homage to all the things its owners hold dear. Rosamund and Bill de la Hey love things that are functional and simply made but look beautiful. They love the quirky and the original. They love people – and dogs. But most of all they love food and books. The shop is, as you would hope, lined floor to ceiling with the most wonderful selection of books for all tastes and all ages. There are hiding places under the stairs where children can tuck themselves away and immerse themselves in an imaginary world. There are unusual cards and gifts, scrubbed wooden tables and mismatched chairs, piles of irresistible cakes and the smell of very, very good coffee. Intrigued by the artistically whimsical window displays, it is the sort of place you might idly wander into and find yourself having to be forcibly removed at closing time.

I didn't give my talk in the bookshop but in one of the collection of buildings behind it, one of which houses the deli – Bill's temple of culinary delights. My event was in an upstairs room absolutely jam-packed with chairs.

'We've sold out!' said Ros in answer to my worried expression. The audience was generous, their questions interesting and fun and after the last book was sold and I had scribbled a grateful signature in it, Bill and Ros raided the deli and took me back to their house for supper. The following day I returned to the bookshop to thank them and say goodbye.

'Please will you choose a book to take away?' said Ros. 'We always like to give our visiting speakers a book to say thank you.'

'That's ridiculously kind and unnecessary,' I replied, 'and I'd love to accept, but will you recommend one? Perhaps by an author I won't be familiar with?'

Without hesitation Ros handed me a paperback by an American writer called Garth Stein. I'd never heard of him. The title, *The Art of Racing in the Rain*, was written in a font that looked like handwriting and on the front cover was a blurred, close-up photograph of part of a dog's face against a vivid blue background.

'Let me know what you think,' said Ros with a smile.

I don't want to tell you too much about the book, as I urge you to read it for yourselves, but the blurb on the cover describes it as 'the captivating and moving story of an extraordinary family, how they almost fell apart and how they were brought back together by the wisest and most loyal member – Enzo the dog'. To be honest, that doesn't really do it justice. It is a story more complex and intricate than that implies and it is really beautifully told, but the reason I bring it up here is because at one point in the story Enzo detects that there is something very wrong with the health of one of the characters, long before she, or anyone else, realises it. He is just the family pet, he has no idea what these unusual signs that he is picking up mean, or how to communicate that he is aware of them, but it is an interesting detail in the story and one that isn't in any way the figment of an author's imagination.

If you happen to read *The Week*, you'll know it is a potted version of the weekly news that includes, among other things, who was the guest on that week's *Desert Island Discs* and what they chose, a précis of *The Archers*, and an invaluable round-up of the main news stories, how they were reported by the different newspapers and what various commentators had to say about them. There is also a section called 'It wasn't all bad' which lists three stories that will bring back some of your optimism that has leached away while reading the headline news. During a week in January 2015 when the general election campaign got underway with its usual sniping, and the euro was on the verge of collapse yet again, there was also a report about a dog called Ted.

Ted was a two-year-old rescue collie who had been re-homed by Josie Conlan in Stockton-on-Tees. Ted, who had been badly abused as a puppy, was not inclined to be very affectionate towards his new owner but then his behaviour mysteriously changed. Josie recalled that he started to whimper and paw at her chest, as if trying to communicate with her that something was wrong. When she put her hand to her chest, she discovered she had a lump in her breast, which, when she went to a doctor, transpired to be a particularly virulent form of cancer. Thanks to Ted, the lump was discovered before the cancer spread. She is in no doubt that her life was saved by her dog.

Josie and Ted

Claire Guest nodded with recognition when I recounted this story. Some years before, a friend and colleague of hers called Gill, then in her early twenties, told Claire that her dog had started to persistently lick and sniff at a mole on her leg. As far as Gill was concerned this was an unchanging mole and nothing to worry about, but her dog became obsessed with it, to the point that even if she walked past the dog when it was asleep, it would wake up and go straight to the mole on her leg. It transpired that it was cancerous, but at an early enough stage to be treated successfully. Claire, who had studied psychology and animal behaviour, was Director of Operations and Research at what was then a very new charity – Hearing Dogs for Deaf People. In the course of her studies and her work she had heard anecdotal evidence that dogs seemed to be able to detect cancer, but Gill's experience got her thinking. If dogs really did have an ability to detect cancer at very early stages, the implications could be tremendous, but it needed to be proved by rigorous scientific investigation. Claire started to approach the cancer research charities and people in the medical profession, but the idea was met with what she described as 'a wall of scepticism'. No one was interested. 'I thought they would bite my hand off! But it was quite the opposite.' She almost let the idea go when Gill came rushing into her office and said, 'You'll never guess who I've heard on Radio 4! Dr John Church! We've got to get in touch with him.'

Dr John Church was an orthopaedic surgeon who came to prominence as the primary force behind the introduction of maggot therapy programmes for wound care in the

UK. While being interviewed on Radio 4, he also happened to mention his interest in what appeared to be the ability of dogs to spot cancer in their owners. He had even written to the medical journal the *Lancet* on the subject. He ended with an appeal. 'If anybody out there thinks they could train a dog for me to try and prove this, could they come forward.'

It was exactly the impetus Claire needed. She had been involved in the training of dogs for tasks involving scent for many years and was confident that if cancer proved to have an odour detectable by dogs, she could train them to recognise it. She met with John and in 2002 they did their first study in collaboration with the Buckinghamshire NHS Trust. But this was pioneering stuff. No one had done it before. In drug detection, as I'd seen with Aran and Mike, a dog is trained on a sample of the drugs it will be looking for, so it can become absolutely familiar with the scent of that particular chemical compound. But when Claire started her initial study, no one knew what it was that made some dogs aware that something was amiss with their owners. They weren't even sure that cancer had a detectable smell. All Claire and John could do was try using samples from known cancer patients, aware that it wouldn't necessarily be a pure sample, that it could be complicated by other things like an infection or blood in the urine that may also have a smell. Somehow they would have to train the dogs to ignore those smells and only indicate on the one common factor in the samples – cancer.

When she told me this I have to say I started to appreciate why her idea had been greeted with such scepticism.

It seemed an absolutely impossible task. But Claire, as I was to discover when I went to meet her in Milton Keynes, is clearly not someone who gives up easily. She radiates a sense of purpose that is utterly beguiling. Driven entirely by the belief that if they could prove a dog's ability to smell cancer it would save lives, she and John worked and worked until they had clinically robust data. Published in the *British Medical Journal* in 2004, their research indicated two game-changing facts: cancer has an odour and dogs can be trained to find it.

'Wow, what a welcome!' I laughed. Claire and I had walked into the office of Rob Harris, who left his job training drug-detection dogs to join Claire at Medical Detection Dogs, the charity she set up in 2007. I was greeted by a pack of excited dogs and the strong whiff of warm Labrador.

'We have a no-kennel policy,' explained Claire. 'We believed right from the start that to allow this fantastic relationship we're developing with dogs, it's essential that we live and work together. Most of the dogs were working breeds like Labradors and spaniels that come from all different backgrounds. Some are donated. One little dog, Martha, was a rescue dog that had been dumped at the side of a road, so riddled with mange she was completely bald. There are also guide dogs that have failed to make the grade because they are "visually distracted".'

The main reason dogs are visually distracted, as Claire explained, is because they want to smell things. As I'd learnt from Penny, guide dogs can't give in to their sniffing impulses. But it is this desire to sniff that makes these dogs so invaluable to Claire and Rob.

Next to Rob's office is the training room which is dominated by a sort of carousel with arms radiating out from the middle, all set at dog-nose height. I was introduced to Daisy, an English Springer Spaniel, who lives with a local family, along with two young children and another dog.

'So the dogs you work with don't live here all the time?' I asked.

Rob shook his head. 'No, it's really important that they don't. The kennel environment for our type of dogs doesn't suit them, they like to be with people, they like to be around people, they want to work with people.'

'So these are dogs with day jobs?'

'Exactly that. We like to say they come in on the school run!'

Small sample pots were placed at the end of each arm of the carousel, one of them containing a urine sample from a man with prostate cancer. Rob stood behind a one-way screen so that he could see the dog, but the dog couldn't see him. This helps avoid Rob inadvertently giving a signal to the dog that might give away which sample is the contaminated one. Daisy was given the command and quick as a flash she smelt one, two, three, four of the samples and then stopped and sat down by the fifth.

'Has she got it right?' I asked Rob. She had, and it had taken a matter of seconds. Daisy continued to get it right, even when new samples were put in place.

Claire and Rob have successfully trained a team of ten of their dogs to find amyl acetate, which smells like pear drops. Most humans can smell amyl acetate diluted by one part per five hundred; the best human noses can detect it at one part per thousand – the equivalent, say, of a millilitre of cordial in a litre of water. Claire asked me to guess what the results of their study showed. Given what I'd learnt about dogs' noses I thought I was in a position to make a relatively educated attempt. 'One part per ten million?' I ventured.

'Well,' said Claire, 'we did find they varied in ability, just like humans, but they all got a bit lower than that, didn't they, Rob?'

Rob grinned. 'The best dogs got down to one part per trillion. And we couldn't go any lower than one part per trillion here because the scientist who was preparing the samples didn't have the equipment to do it.'

'It's one of the things we wanted to assess here,' explained Claire. 'How low could our dogs go in terms of detection levels? How sensitive are they?'

My jaw dropped. Claire laughed. 'We couldn't believe it either! This wasn't like our previous medical studies – it was purely to see what a dog's nose might be capable of, but it unleashes another whole range of possibilities.'

The next three or four years will be spent gathering what Claire describes as a 'massive evidence base' with which they can go back to consultants to demonstrate the reliability of dogs' rate of detection of conditions like prostate cancer. At the moment one of the methods used by the medical profession to detect cancer in urine samples is a device called the electronic nose, but it is nothing like as sensitive as a dog's nose and takes a couple of hours to screen six samples, whereas a dog can do five times that in just five minutes. What Claire hopes is that if the research they do over the next few years does continue to demonstrate that dogs can accurately detect cancer – and different forms of cancer at that – dog detection could be used alongside the electronic nose to help consultants get earlier accurate diagnoses.

'So was the turning point as a result of that first scientific trial you published in 2004? Was that what brought the medical profession around?'

Claire looked rueful. The 2004 study created a lot of interest and prompted more studies around the world, some of them good, but some of them, as Claire put it diplomatically, 'not so good'. She, in the meantime, had left the security of her job with Hearing Dogs and taken the bold step of setting up her charity, Medical Detection Dogs. But the medical profession and cancer charities continued to be resistant to what she was trying to do, funding was hard to come by and just a few months after setting up the charity her marriage fell apart.

'I had no idea what rock bottom meant until that point,' Claire said quietly. 'I had such bad reactive depression. I couldn't do anything any more. I literally felt my life was over. But my family, my friends, people like Rob, just kept saying, "Don't let it go, you've got to keep trying." And it was their belief and support that kept me going and then this thing happened with Daisy...'

I had spent much of my day at Medical Detection Dogs in a state of awe, admiration and sheer disbelief, but what Clare went on to tell me left me dumbstruck. Daisy was a five-year-old dog that Claire was working with on bladder cancer trials. At the end of every day, Daisy and a couple of other dogs involved in the work would go home with Claire. As usual she stopped to give them a run around on the way home. Two of the dogs jumped out of the car but Daisy stayed put. 'She kept on jumping at me and staring at me with her big brown eyes and then she pushed against me about two or three times. And I pushed her off and said, "Daisy, what's the matter? Go away." But she did it again until I finally persuaded her to get out of the car. And then for some reason I put my hand up to my chest and realised I had a funny bruise there. Nothing you could see, but you know, one of those deep bruises you can feel.'

Claire thought nothing of it until a couple of days later when she felt it again and there seemed to be a bit of a lump there. Her doctor was concerned enough to refer her immediately to a consultant.

'I think it's a cyst,' the consultant said, 'but I'll do a biopsy anyway.' It did indeed prove to be a cyst, but there was an area that concerned doctors so they asked her to go to hospital and have core biopsies. They showed cancer.

'When the consultant broke the news to me he said I was incredibly lucky because it was a very deep cancer and by the time it had grown big enough to feel, it would have been too late and my prognosis very poor. As I was only forty-five, I was not due to be called for a mammogram for another five years, which would have been too late.'

'Did you tell your consultant that it was your dog that alerted you to the fact that something was wrong?'

'I didn't on the day of the diagnosis, but I did later, and he admitted to being very sceptical. He now works with

Medical Detection Dogs as the principal investigator on our breast cancer study!'

'And how about you? How did it affect you?'

'At that point, it really didn't look like the work we were doing with cancer was going to go anywhere. There was simply too much resistance. But Daisy detected my cancer and saved me, and I thought, "Who else could it save?" I knew then I couldn't give up.'

And she didn't. Medical Detection Dogs' work to investigate the possible capabilities of dogs to be able to diagnose all sorts of conditions at very early stages are now, at last, being given serious consideration. A trial is underway to ascertain whether breast cancer is detectable by odour, and the charity has also been asked to run tests to see whether dogs are able to detect the very early signs of Parkinson's disease. Currently Parkinson's can only be diagnosed when damage to the brain has already occurred. But Parkinson's sufferers develop a slightly greasy skin, which is quite clear when the disease is in the advanced stages. If dogs are able to detect something in the sebaceous glands that appears to be abnormal, this may be a way of discovering whether someone is going to develop Parkinson's before damage to the brain occurs. If that's the case, the medication currently used to slow down the progress of the disease could hold back the damage occurring to the brain. Dogs could once again prove to be an invaluable partner to humans in a way that just a few short years ago hardly anyone would ever have dared to believe.

Chapter 17
A Friend For Life

Hamish, Jess and Doug

A dog is the only thing on earth that loves you more than he loves himself.

Josh Billings, American humorist

So it seems that even after all the thousands of years we have lived and worked with dogs, they still have the capacity to surprise us. Even dogs like Harvey Nics, trained to be an assistance dog, demonstrated that he was capable of doing something that no one realised dogs could do. Harvey Nics is a golden-coloured miniature labradoodle, with a personality that more than makes up for his lack of stature, and the ability to make everyone smile, particularly his owner, Lizzie. Lizzie has had curvature of the spine since childhood and a later accident left her needing to use a wheelchair. Harvey Nics helps Lizzie with the shopping by getting things off supermarket shelves and paying at the check-out. He'll put things away in drawers and retrieve them when needed, help her dress and undress and load the washing machine. 'He even taught himself to separate the lights from the darks!' laughs Lizzie.

But Harvey Nics started to do something that he hadn't been trained to do. For no apparent reason, one night he woke Lizzie up. 'He just nudged me awake and then sat looking intently at me.' A couple of days later Lizzie had a routine asthma check and was told that her peak flow – the rate air can be expelled from the lungs – was dangerously low, indicating she could have a major attack at any time. Was Harvey Nics' uncharacteristic behaviour linked in any way to Lizzie's condition? Had he somehow picked up that something was wrong? Lizzie wasn't sure, but when he did the same thing a few weeks later, she checked her peak flow and found that once again it was right down. 'He always seems to know and he has never been wrong.'

No one knows why dogs seem to be aware when something is amiss. Friederike Range at the Wolf Science Center believes that what dogs react to is something that is weird, something that is different from the norm, but she doesn't go as far as thinking that the dog actually understands that there is something wrong. 'When I was pregnant, the wolves reacted to that. They came up to me, and were sniffing at me. They could smell a change. Similarly, if a dog picks up a smell from its owner that is different, that is uncharacteristic, it is going to make it nervous. It is likely that it will go up and nuzzle the person, to be able to check that smell more closely. There is a sensitivity there when a human and dog are bonded, the relationship is important, so they are going to be looking for reassurance.'

I asked Claire Guest what she thought. She pondered for a bit. 'Does a dog pick up on a potential danger or just on something different? Truthfully, we don't know the answer but we have two ideas that might help to explain it.'

Her first theory – 'the nicer one!' – is based on how pack animals behave. 'There's a lot of evidence now that the pack leader will be protected by a coalition of other pack members, so that younger animals aren't constantly challenging his position. There is support among the pack, because that is essential for the pack's survival, and it may be that if an animal smells something different, picks up on an odour that indicates a change in health of a fellow pack member, that they would protect that vulnerable animal. A dog that is bonded with a human being may also be reacting in a protective way when it becomes aware that that person is smelling different.'

'And the other idea?' I asked.

'Well, it could be a bit more sinister, and hark back to their wolf ancestry,' laughed Claire. 'Any predator hunting prey is going to want to conserve energy as much as they possibly can, so they will go for the weaker animals like youngsters, or the ones that are not in the peak of health. Being able to identify weakness in their prey would make hunting a lot easier.'

That is a trait I have certainly seen in sheepdogs. Hamish and Susie Dykes farm sheep and cattle on the Scottish Borders. Hamish has two Huntaways, a breed that I had never come across before. They come from New Zealand, where they are much prized as herding dogs. Intelligent and agile, with endless stamina, they have been bred to work on vast sheep stations, where there are few fences and the ground is steep and rough. The characteristic that really identifies them as Huntaways is their bark. I went out with Hamish on a beautiful autumn day to see his two, Jess and Doug, at work. In the yard the dogs are as soppy as much-loved family pets. Doug, huge and handsome, was clearly used to being admired and Jess, his mum, tried to steal back the limelight first by rolling over at my feet inviting me to scratch her tummy and then standing up and leaning her full and not inconsiderable weight against my legs, while I was talking to Hamish. But out on the hill, with a flock of wily Scottish Blackface sheep needing to be gathered up and brought in, I understood why these dogs are becoming increasingly popular. Both dogs were trembling with the anticipation of the task ahead, and as soon as Hamish brought the quad bike to a halt they were off.

'Speak up!' Hamish called and they started to bark. Welsh dogs are also expected to bark when working sheep or cattle, but they may only bark occasionally. Huntaways bark almost constantly, a deep, resonating sound that drives the sheep out from the hidden dips and crevices. The hillside Jess and Doug were working was rough and full of tussocks, rocks and boggy patches, and the sheep were scattered across it as far as the eye could see. Yet as soon as they heard the barks their heads were up and they were on the move. Almost before I reached the summit of the hill to get a view of the action, the dogs had gathered the sheep and were driving them in a long woolly line towards the gate.

'That'll do!' said Hamish, as he closed the gate on the last of the stragglers and the air was suddenly heavy with silence.

But a good sheepdog will also be invaluable when it comes to helping a shepherd catch a single animal out of the flock. A few months later, in March, Hamish and I went out with the dogs to check on the ewes. They were all in lamb and some had started to give birth. His experienced eye spotted a problem with one of them. She was in labour, but only one leg had come out, a sure sign that the other front leg was tucked back preventing the ewe pushing the lamb out. She would need help delivering it, but ewes are remarkably quick on their feet, even in the throes of giving birth, and they pay no heed at all to the fact that you might be trying to help them. Not only that, they have an unerring talent for getting themselves into the thick of the flock and disappearing. In a twenty-acre field this ewe would have been nigh on impossible to catch if not for the dogs. Almost the moment Hamish had spotted her, it seemed the dogs had too and they had no problem splitting her off from the rest of the flock and standing guard so that

Hamish could run in and catch her. Teg has also proudly shown me that she can identify and single out the sheep with a bad foot, or some other problem, although I've never trained her to do it. Is it that inherent instinct that enables dogs not just to sniff out cancer but the onset of something like an asthma attack? And if they could do that, and be trained to do it reliably, was this another way that humans could glean huge benefit from an association with dogs? Claire and her colleagues believed it could be.

The research and training they had done to establish whether dogs could identify cancer had also demonstrated that dogs would pick up on other conditions. As well as using samples from known cancer patients to train the dogs, they would mix them up with healthy samples and later with samples of people with other diseases that were not cancer. Even though the dogs would only indicate on the cancer samples, they would always react to the other samples that were not healthy. 'We were becoming increasingly aware that these other diseases seemed to give off biochemical changes that the dogs were detecting.' Not only that, they were hearing more and more stories of people like Lizzie who believed their dogs might be picking up on something that allowed them to predict the onset of things like asthma attacks or epileptic fits. Then Claire was approached by a woman in Durham whose husband had a very brittle form of type 1 diabetes. He managed his condition very well and very carefully, but in common with ten per cent of other long-term diabetics he suffers from hyperglycaemic unawareness. This means his body no longer notices when his blood sugar is dangerously low, and he can literally be walking down the street and fall into a coma with no prior warning. This was happening to her husband every day; he was going into hospital two or three times a week, and because he was also on blood thinners, if he cut himself when he fell, his blood wouldn't clot.

'I was so worried whenever he went anywhere on his own,' his wife told Claire. She had read that there were diabetic alert dogs being used in Australia and America but there didn't seem to be any in the UK. Did Claire think there was anything she could do to help?

Claire went up and stayed for a few days with the family. The family already had a dog, Zeta, which they had puppy-walked during her training as a guide dog. When she failed to pass as a guide dog, they had given her a home. Claire asked if they had noticed any changes in Zeta's behaviour before the husband had a hyperglycaemic attack. 'No,' they said, 'there's no change at all.'

But Claire's experience of studying canine behaviour told her something different. Throughout the days Claire watched Zeta as she sat with the husband and he regularly checked his blood levels. When they got low, Claire noticed that Zeta seemed to stare at him. 'It was just slightly,' said Claire, 'and the family hadn't noticed it, but I started to reward her with a treat every time she did it. Quickly she realised that she got a treat when she stared and started to stare in a more noticeable way. And every time she stared I asked the husband to check his blood sugar levels and every time it was dipping.'

'But surely,' I said, 'if she realised that she would get a

treat every time she stared, she would just stare for no reason at all, wouldn't she?'

Claire shook her head. 'You might get a little bit of them trying it on, but they realise very quickly if you train them right and you reward them for a behaviour they were already doing. Within just three or four weeks this dog was working with almost a hundred per cent reliability. She completely changed that man's life.'

Since that breakthrough moment in 2008, over sixty more dogs have been trained to alert their diabetic owners to the onset of a hyperglycaemic attack, including Shirley, a rather beautiful Golden Retriever/Labrador cross. She goes with her young owner, Rebecca, to school every day and will wake Rebecca's mum in the night if she detects that Rebecca's blood sugar is getting too low. And with the success of these dogs came publicity and more requests from desperate people and their families to see if a dog could change their lives too. And they weren't just people with diabetes. Claire and her team were once again entering uncharted territory.

'No one in the world had done or was doing what we were doing,' said Claire, 'but we are all experienced trainers with a good understanding of canine behaviour and a strong belief that dogs can do almost anything.' So when Claire was asked to help Kelly, a teenager with chronic and debilitating narcolepsy, they set out to achieve a world first. Kelly had an understandably bleak view of her future, one where she wouldn't be able to live independently, go to work or go out alone. She falls asleep several times a day, with no warning. This is very different from nodding off after a heavy lunch, or catching forty winks on the train into work after a late night. Imagine walking up the stairs and suddenly falling asleep as you reach the top. That happened to Kelly and she woke up covered in cuts and bruises back at the bottom of the staircase. But what would give a dog a sign or a clue that Kelly was about to have an attack? Even humans, with their inferior noses, can pick up a change of smell in urine, which might indicate diabetes, but does falling asleep have a smell? It turned out that it does, or at least, the chemical changes that occur just before falling asleep do, as long as you have the supersensitive nose of Theo the Cocker Spaniel. Theo was trained to recognise those chemical changes and alert Kelly to them by licking her hand. That warning gives her a chance to sit down, or get herself somewhere safe before she falls asleep. Theo will get help if she does fall and wake her up by licking her face. They've had similar successes with people suffering from Addison's disease, when dogs can alert before the onset of a potentially fatal drop in cortisol levels; and for people with PoTS (postural tachycardia syndrome), which causes them to have frequent debilitating and often dangerous blackouts.

'How do you do it?' I asked, incredulous. 'Can you just train a dog to recognise a certain thing and pair it up with anyone who happens to have that condition, or is it more personal than that? Does the bond between owner and dog have to be established and strong for this to work?'

'Sometimes we can train dogs people already have, like in the case of Zeta,' said Claire, 'but otherwise the way we do it is to train a dog to a certain scent, so we will collect the scent of someone with low blood sugar, or low cortisol levels in the case of someone with Addison's, and teach the dog that that is the scent we are interested in. Once we know they recognise that scent, we will start to train them to the smell of the person we are planning to pair them up with.'

She told me about Claire Moon, a nurse working at a hospital in Cambridge. Claire and her team look after three hundred children and young people, offering them care, support and advice on how they and their families can cope with diabetes. And Claire is particularly well qualified to do the job because she too has had diabetes since she was a teenager. She goes to work in the company of a golden Labrador called Magic and everyone loves him. 'He makes the clinic a happy and welcoming place. And this effect has spread, not just through the children's diabetes clinic, but wherever Claire goes in the hospital.' But Magic is not at the hospital as a therapy dog for the patients. He is there to alert Claire when her blood sugar dips.

'But what about all the other patients in the ward? They must often have low blood glucose levels too?'

Claire nodded. 'It is truly amazing, but that dog never alerts to anyone else, only Claire. Once they learn the scent we want them to recognise, we train the dog only on the scent of the person they are going to be matched with. And so by the time it meets the person, they would have smelt them every day for a few days and they sort of recognise them – it's a bit like you or me having seen hundreds of photos of a person and then meeting them in the flesh. You think you know them.'

But after that, the long-term success of the partnership will be down to the bond. 'It sounds a bit unscientific, but we look for these sort of emotional matches, that somehow just work. And if we get that right and we get the scent training right, most of our dogs alert within the first twenty-four hours with their new owner.'

Tara Bedford's partner, Emma, presented Claire with her most challenging project to date. Tara and Emma live in Oxfordshire with their Jack Russell terrier, Widjet (it's with a 'j' not a 'g', I was told, politely but firmly). One evening some years ago, Tara was having dinner with her parents when she had an allergic reaction to a chocolate brownie. It had nuts in it, but, as Tara told me over the phone, she had always eaten nuts as a child, they always had nuts on the table at Christmas, so she assumed it must be a reaction to something else. She didn't bother to have any tests because she thought it was probably a one-off. It wasn't. She continued to suffer from increasingly severe allergic reactions and when she did finally go to get tested it was confirmed that somehow, mysteriously, she had developed a sensitivity to nuts. 'But I was still able to go to restaurants and eat out and things like that, and other people around me could eat nuts and it would be fine.'

But then Tara had a couple of reactions for what appeared to be no discernible reason. 'It was very confusing. I was working at a nursery at the time and one of the other staff was eating a Snickers bar in the staffroom and I had a reaction. It seemed that just being in the same room as someone else eating nuts could cause me to go into anaphylactic shock.'

I tried to gather my thoughts. Could someone who had no previous sensitivity to nuts suddenly develop an allergy so extreme they couldn't even be in the same room as someone or something that had come into contact with nuts? According to Tara's consultant, it can happen, but it is very rare. Rare it may be, but it turned Tara's life upside-down. Every reaction – and they were becoming more and more frequent because she was allergic to something she couldn't know was there – would wipe her out for days afterwards. She was constantly in and out of A & E and it became pretty much impossible to carry on doing the job she loved.

'I hope you don't think I'm being insensitive,' I asked, 'but can you give me an idea of how this has affected your life?'

'Since 2008 I've been on antidepressants and had lots of counselling, but it is still very hard,' Tara replied. 'I loved my job, but couldn't carry on it with it any more. I couldn't go out to restaurants or the cinema. I couldn't go on planes or stay in hotels. It put a huge amount of pressure on Emma. I felt guilty for having the allergy.'

She and Emma had got to their wits' end. 'We thought there must be something we can do, something that can give me part of my life back.' It was Emma who had the idea to find out if a dog could provide the solution. She wrote to numerous charities in the UK that work with dogs and was directed along a path that eventually led her to Claire. For a dog to be able to prevent Tara having an anaphylactic reaction it would have to be able to detect the presence of nuts in the air – a mere trace of a scent

– and alert her to the fact that that place wasn't safe for her to go into. No one in the world had ever trained a dog to do that. No one knew if it was possible. In response to Emma's enquiry, Claire said, 'We could give it a try and see what happens.'

'Forgive the bad pun,' I said to Tara, 'but did you think Emma – and indeed Claire – were barking mad?'

Tara confessed that she didn't really take it all in. She knew that in America there were nut-detection dogs that could support someone who was touch and taste sensitive, but, she said, 'I wasn't a hundred per cent sure how the airborne side would work. I think Claire and her team were a bit stumped too, but they found a way, because now I have Willow.'

It certainly wasn't all plain sailing. In the early days of Willow's training, things didn't progress as well as everyone hoped and Tara, who had dared to get her hopes up, dared to imagine being able to go out and do things, was often reduced to tears when it seemed that what Willow was being asked to do was indeed impossible. But then, all of a sudden, a few months into training, Willow seemed to understand what was being asked of her and she was introduced to Tara for the first time. That all-important bond that Claire had told me about was evident almost from the outset. 'She just kept coming up to me, watching me all the time. She didn't take her eyes off me.' So the bond was there, but then they had to train Willow how to indicate to Tara that she could detect traces of the scent that would cause a reaction.

'It had to be quite forceful and obvious so that I could

respond immediately. She will physically push me back sometimes.'

But Willow needed to have an equally strong bond with Tara's partner Emma, because most of the time they will go out together. 'Emma and Willow will go ahead of me into a room and Willow will walk around, nose in the air, tail wagging, smelling everywhere and taking Emma along with her. If she does smell something, she will alert Emma and I won't go any further.'

Tara's life is still restricted, but she has started working again – teaching swimming in a school where everyone knows about her condition and makes sure that they have nothing with them that could trigger a reaction. She has also enrolled on an Open University degree course studying history. She still suffers from anaphylactic shocks when there is a certain sort of pollen in the atmosphere, but, she told me, 'Having Willow by my side has really helped. She never leaves me. She'll check the doctors, the medication. She is a real comfort, especially because I know after suffering an attack I'm going to be feeling absolutely rotten for the next few days.'

Tara's consultant is hopeful that Tara's condition may yet become less severe, that it might revert to being a touch and taste allergy. If that happened, I wondered, would that make Willow redundant?

'I don't know,' replied Tara. 'I'm hoping that she would still stay with me and not go to someone else. The bond between us is so strong. She follows me everywhere, no matter what I'm doing. She boosts my confidence and gets me through. I would be destroyed if she had to go.'

Claire and her team had defied scepticism, negativity, rejection and once again proved beyond all doubt that dogs can support humans in ways that no one would ever have imagined possible. 'Are there limits to what dogs could do in this field?' I asked Claire.

'Maybe!' she laughed. 'But we haven't found them yet.'

I headed home. It takes a long time to drive from Milton Keynes to Wales during the evening rush hour. The 'Mna Mna' song from *The Muppets* was playing on the radio – the signature tune of Simon Mayo's *All Request Friday*. When I was a child *The Muppets* was essential Saturday-afternoon viewing for my whole family. If I wanted to make my dad laugh, I would sing him the 'Mna Mna' song. Now, I slightly blush to admit, I sing it to my dogs. Did early humans sing? I mused to myself as I dropped down into second gear and joined a crawling line of traffic. And if they did, did they ever sing to their attendant wolves? Or did singing to dogs evolve later, perhaps after a successful hunt? Did the Thule serenade the dogs pulling their sledges? The seal hunter who'd driven my sledge in Greenland didn't sing, but maybe I'd cramped his style. Scott and Shackleton wouldn't have sung to their dogs, I'm sure, but I like to think that Amundsen was moved to break into a rousing Norwegian number in praise of his dogs when they reached the South Pole. Even if it is just me that sings to my dogs (and I gather it's not, because lots of you confessed on Twitter to doing the same), I know I'm not alone when I say I feel better when there is a dog around. And as many people I have met and talked to in the course of my research have attested, human beings often do better with the help of a dog. In the early days of the relationship, dogs allowed humans to feel safe, to hunt more successfully, to travel greater distances. Dogs protected our possessions, and still do, found people that were lost, and still do, can act as our eyes, our ears, support us, comfort us, even save our lives. I remember my final question to Friederike Range before I left the Wolf Science Center. I asked if she thought our association with dogs had evolved to such a point that we now couldn't live without them.

'We could live without them,' she said, 'but it wouldn't be so nice!'

But I wonder. I wonder if we really could? Ask Marjory to speak on behalf of all those who have had guide dogs, ask the shepherds in the Wakhan Corridor or the Mongolian desert or in Wales. Ask the family of Genelle Guzman, found by a dog, alive, buried under forty feet of concrete in the aftermath of the attacks on the World Trade Center. Ask those who served on the front line in Afghanistan, the parents of autistic children. Ask Jon Flint and the people with chronic, life-threatening illnesses. Ask the young men serving time at Polmont Young Offenders Institution. Ask conservationists and customs officers. Ask the carers of the elderly, the lonely, the vulnerable, and I suspect they might all feel differently. Yes, the human race could exist without dogs but it would be a lot worse off without them. Even if we take Greger Larson's most conservative estimate, our relationship with dogs has developed over at least fifteen thousand years, and Claire Guest believes it is a relationship that still has much, much more it can offer.

'Dogs have evolved alongside us. They've become highly attuned to us, so much so that they can read our facial expressions and our emotions. And at last we are starting to realise that we can understand more about our relationship with dogs – and get more from it – by sitting back and letting them take the lead. We've realised that we can work things out more effectively when we work in partnership. We are better at some things and they are better at others. Work together and suddenly the potential is massive.'

Chapter 18

Two Feet, Four Paws: An Extraordinary Partnership

Me and Teg

I like a bit of mongrel myself, whether it's a man or a dog; they're the best for everyday.

George Bernard Shaw, Irish dramatist, in *Misalliance*

And what of my fledgling partnership with Teg? When we left Dewi's farm I was so buoyed up with happiness, so delighted by what Dewi had said about her, I turned up the radio and sung most of the way home. It is a long drive – about four hours – and after a while I started to get a bit hoarse and Teg gave me an imploring look which said, all too clearly, 'Enough!'

'Good day?' said Ludo, as I pranced into the kitchen, bursting to tell him what had happened. Ludo has always been doubtful of my plans for Teg. I don't think he has ever been entirely convinced that she and I were destined for shepherding greatness and I'm pretty sure he harbours the suspicion that I used an apparent interest in learning to work a dog, just so I could get another one.

'Honestly,' I babbled, 'she was just brilliant. Dewi was really taken by her. I'll show you at the farm tomorrow.'

The following evening an email came through from Adeline. The subject was 'date of the next assessment'. I wrote back. 'I can't do it. I can't take Teg, we're just not ready. We'll both completely let you down.' I was feeling utterly despondent. That day Ludo had stood by and watched as Teg had gone through Tim's sheep like a delinquent. She'd raced through the middle of them, split a group off and chased them down, snapping at their rumps. She had then sped back to the main flock, which scattered to the four winds leaving her – and me – with no clue how to rectify the situation. And almost worst of all, she hadn't listened to any of my commands. I might as well have not been there. If we'd ever had any sort of bond, it had been a fleeting one, a fluke, and there was absolutely no evidence of it now. Ludo was generous enough not to say anything but he didn't need to, his face said it all. And he was right. This whole idea had been one big delusion from the start.

'Nonsense!' replied Adeline. 'Dewi phoned me and told me what she had done. He was genuinely impressed. Dogs aren't machines, they have bad days as well as good ones. The assessment isn't for a couple of weeks. Go up and see Alun Jones. It'll be a good experience for you both.'

Alun lives with his wife and family on a farm in North Wales. The house and farm buildings sit on a slim piece of flat land sandwiched between the road and the mountains that dominate the skyline behind. I met Alun in the yard with his son Morgan and a couple of other men, professional shepherds who travel with their dogs to farms when they need help with the gathers. Sheep on farms like Alun's spend most of the year out on the mountain, free to roam over several hundred acres. Three or four times a year they will be brought down to the farm for jobs like shearing or to be sorted and taken to market. The gathers are a bit of an event and there was an air of anticipation among the little knot of people in the yard. The dogs seemed to pick up on it too. There would be six of them working the hill and they milled around, or sat on the back of the quad bikes, impatient for the off. There were no collies here. This was a purely Welsh affair. The dogs were Welsh, the people were Welsh, the language was Welsh, but far from making me feel like an outsider, they couldn't have been kinder and more hospitable towards me. I hoped their generosity would extend to my dog.

'She's never done anything like this before,' I explained.

'I have no idea what she might do. Are you sure she won't cause any trouble?'

'We've got a plan,' said Alun. 'You see that place up there where the old stone enclosure is?' and he gestured up the hill to a level area above the farm. 'If you wait there with Teg, that's where we bring the sheep to before we drive them down to the pens at the bottom. Teg can help drive them to the pens and bring the ones we want back to the farm. If she goes a bit wild we've got plenty of dogs here to bring the sheep back, so don't worry.'

Teg and I walked up the hill. Alun and the rest had gone ahead on the quad bikes and were climbing right up to the ridgeline. When I got to my spot near the stone enclosure, I scanned the horizon. Some of the quads had disappeared from view; I could just make out one of them in the far distance and the dark outline of a dog racing around a rocky outcrop, flushing sheep out and driving them down the hill. Suddenly there seemed to be sheep coming from every direction, pouring down the mountainside towards me. Teg was on her feet, every muscle tense, straining at her lead, desperate to join in. Alun waved from just below me. 'Let her go!' he shouted. Teg tore down the mountain and into the fray. There were dogs and sheep everywhere. I ran down as fast as I could but I also wanted to watch what was going on.

At first Teg seemed to approach the whole thing like it was one huge game, but gradually I could see she was taking a lead from the other dogs, watching where they were going and what they were doing. She was thinking, working it out and, along with the other dogs, she kept the sheep together and drove them into the field beside the pens. As I ran down the final bit of the slope to join them, dogs and sheep were having a breather, panting hard. The dogs lay at their masters' feet as the men swigged from bottles of water and passed around packets of biscuits. 'She did OK,' said Alun. I've never seen Teg look happier. It was as if she'd found her vocation, that all that poncing about in little fields with a handful of sheep had never been something to take seriously. This was the real deal. This, she seemed to be saying as she flopped delightedly at my feet, is what I was bred for.

When everyone had got their breath back and the biscuits were finished, Alun said, 'We'll keep our dogs out and you see if you and Teg can get the sheep in the pens. This bit is fenced so they can't go too far.'

The pens were on a small area of level ground but the rest of the field was on a steep slope, with a boggy stream running along the bottom corner of it. Teg made a reasonable attempt at trying to gather the sheep, but because neither of us knew the terrain the sheep rather got the better of us and our inexperience started to become more apparent. Alun sent in his dog, Ben, and with Ben's help Teg got the sheep into the pens. Once they were sorted and the ones that weren't coming down to the farm were let back out on to the mountain, Teg and I joined everyone else to drive the sheep the mile or so down to the farm. By now Teg was calmer; she was going well, working in parallel with the other dogs to keep the sheep together and moving in the same direction.

'She just needs more experience,' said John, one of the

shepherds, whose dog-handling skills were masterful and a joy to watch. 'But she's got all the right ideas. I reckon you've got a good dog there.'

It was high praise and I could feel my resolve returning. Alun's wife and mum had made a huge lunch and we sat outside on the grass in front of the house with big mugs of tea and a table groaning with sandwiches, sausage rolls and more cakes than a village fete. It felt very special to be there, to have been invited to take part with my dog, despite our lack of experience and credentials.

'She seemed to enjoy herself!' said Alun, stroking Teg's head.

'She loved it,' I said. 'She just seemed to be completely at home on the mountain. Given the chance, I think she'd happily stay here with you.'

'Well, if you have to go away and you want her to have a working holiday and get some more experience, I'd be very happy to have her.'

It wasn't an empty gesture; Alun's offer was genuine, and it meant a great deal. It also gave me the confidence to tell Adeline that I would take Teg to the assessment day.

'Good. Remember they are not judging you on whether you and Teg do the job perfectly. There will be other young dogs there too who won't know the ropes yet. What they are looking for is how she works – does she stand upright? Hold her tail up? Does she have a loose or fixed eye? Does she bark? They won't fail her if she splits the sheep up or leaves one behind, but they will if she shows any traits that aren't typical of the Welsh dog.'

Teg and I arrived at the farm of Ian Davies. He, along

with three others, would be assessing the dogs on behalf of the Welsh Sheepdog Society. There were quite a few other people there, some of whom I recognised. Simon Mogford, who had shown me the art of catching feral sheep, was there with a young dog. John Davies, founder of the Society, was there with Will, a dog he'd bred that was already showing lots of promise. I watched Will being put through his paces. A dozen sheep were in a field of about five acres. The assessors looked him over and then asked John to take him round the sheep. As ever, it was sheer pleasure to watch a handler as skilled as John working with his dog. Will is still young, younger than Teg and every bit as keen, but John was able to keep him beautifully controlled, and it was a textbook display of how a Welsh dog should work. The assessors were in no doubt and Will was passed.

I have rarely felt so nervous as I did when Teg and I walked across to the group of stern-faced men who were eyeing her critically. They too were unanimous.

'Looks like she's got some collie in her.'

'I don't know,' I said truthfully, as I was still waiting to hear whether Bronwen had been able to find out any more about Teg's mother Missy. 'But she doesn't work like one.'

They looked sceptical. 'Let's see her then.'

In the hope that Teg would be a little less wild, I had taken her for a ten-kilometre run that morning. It made no difference. For the first five minutes it was all a bit chaotic, the sheep scattered and took refuge in the corner of the field where it was difficult for Teg to get them out. I stayed calm, didn't say anything, let her work it out. Gradually she settled down, got the sheep where she wanted them, drove them towards me and stopped them a few feet from the assessors. I called her off and we walked back to them.

'It takes us a bit of time to find our feet,' I said apologetically.

They looked at each other, their expressions impossible to read. One of them, Erwyd, who Adeline had warned me was particularly tough, said, 'Now that she's calmed down a bit, why don't you have another go?'

This time was better. Teg kept the sheep together and it was a much smoother, less frenetic display. I knew the assessors were all expecting to see a giveaway sign that would prove their suspicions about her ancestry right, and I suspect this second chance was really for them to double-check that Teg didn't suddenly start fixing the sheep with her eyes or tuck her tail down between her legs. She didn't. To my eyes at least she was working as she always does, upright, alert, with that sort of joyful Welsh bounce that is so characteristic.

'I think we may have done her a disservice,' said Ian. 'She showed no collie traits at all.'

'She's passed,' confirmed Erwyd.

A couple of weeks later I pulled up outside Adeline's house. 'Have you heard from Bronwen yet?' she asked, as I climbed out. I nodded. Bronwen had called me the previous week. She had managed to find the diary where she had written the name and number of the man who she had bought Missy from.

'He's a lovely man called Aubrey, farms up in North Wales. I went to see him.'

'And?'

'And Missy's mum was Welsh. He showed me pictures. Looks exactly like Missy, that pale red colour and foxy little ears.'

'And the dad?'

'A really good-looking collie . . .' Adeline laughed. 'Had to be! With a tail like that' – and Teg wagged it as if to make the point – 'It's a dead giveaway.'

'So it seems I am the proud owner of a third mongrel.'

'Yes, but don't forget Teg passed the assessment. We can't register her, because the Society stipulates there are to be no other breeds in the previous two generations. But her puppies can be, as long as you breed her with a registered Welsh dog and they pass the assessment, so you can still do your bit to shore up the future of the Welsh sheepdog. Will you breed from her, do you think?'

'I'm considering it,' I said. 'Aubrey said that if I did he'd like a puppy.'

'Any dog in mind?'

'A couple,' I smiled. 'I think you'll approve. They've all got impeccable Welsh credentials.'

'Right, well, I'm going to leave you to your own devices today. You'll be working the sheep in the top field. Get Teg to bring them down to the lower field and walk them to – say – where the telegraph pole is. Then cross over to the hedge line and drive them up there – you at the front and Teg at the back. Take them back through the gate, but keep about twenty of them with you. I've put the trailer out there, so you can see if you and Teg can load them.'

I walked across the field, my dog beside me. I opened

the gate and we both went through. 'Sit.' Teg sat with her eyes fixed on mine, waiting for the word. The sheep were spread out on the bank above us but a few of them were tucked in under the hawthorn on the field boundary away to the right. Teg would need to head along the bottom of the field and up the line of the hedge to push them out and drive them towards the rest of the flock. I looked down at her, at those lovely mad eyes.

'Away!' She was off, up the bank, but then spotted the sheep in the hedge and changed course. She looked so beautiful, a sleek streak of ginger and white racing full stretch across the field. She flushed the sheep out from the hedgerow and followed them as they ran to join the rest. Then Teg turned uphill again, getting behind the rest of the sheep to drive them down towards me as I waited at the gate. She ran in an arc to and fro, but then, when she had got them about halfway down the field she ran past them, down one side of the flock, pushing them to the left. She stopped. She was looking at me, head cocked on one side. She was checking. Was I concentrating? Was I in control? Did I have the front of the flock?

'I've got them, Teg. Get back!' And she turned back, gathered them up again and brought them down to the gate. I swung it open and let them through. I walked ahead towards the telegraph pole in the middle of the field, my body half turned towards the sheep, watching them, watching Teg. Between us we kept them on track, moving purposefully, me being the steadying anchor at the front, Teg being the gentle driving force at the back. At the pole we turned them and made our way to the hedge. They fanned out along the boundary, Teg keeping them in check at the back as I led them to the gate. I let most of them through, keeping a small bunch behind. Teg was there in a flash, stopping them bolting after the others and keeping them together. We worked our way down the field towards the trailer that Adeline had parked alongside the fence. We were moving seamlessly now, we had a rhythm, it was almost as if we were dancing a well-rehearsed routine. Teg knew what to do, I knew where to be, the sheep were our chorus line. I hadn't asked Teg to do anything. I didn't need to. Each of us knew what we had to do to help the other. This was it. This was the feeling that I had been striving for, an unbeatable, joyous sensation, when I realised I had attained the trust and understanding of my dog and that we were a partnership.

'Please,' I said silently, to no one in particular, 'when I'm old and dribbly and can't recall my own name, let me remember this moment.'

We got to the trailer and Teg drove the sheep around the back so that they were in front of the ramp. This was going to be tricky. Sheep don't like to feel cornered, don't want to be pushed into a space they can't see a way out of. It can make them want to bolt or be belligerent or both. I was standing at the hurdles on the other side of the trailer, holding my crook outwards, trying to help Teg create a funnel that would persuade the sheep the only way to go was forwards. Gradually I eased the hurdles inwards as Teg drove the sheep ahead. A few started up the ramp and then a couple – and there is always a couple – baulked at going any further and all at once the sheep that were already in the trailer seemed to want to make their escape and the others at the bottom of the ramp looked to try and turn tail and run for it. Teg and I needed to stand firm and stay calm. Teg looked at me as if to say, 'I need you to do more than just stand there.' I shouted and waved my arms. She barked. The sheep thought the better of it and walked up the ramp.

Adeline, who had been watching from the gate, walked over to join us. She was smiling. So was I.

'Bet that felt good!' she said.

'It really, really did!'

'I'll go and put the kettle on to celebrate. Will you and Teg take this lot back to the top field to join the rest of them?'

As the last of the sheep ran through the gate I called my dog. 'That'll do, Teg.' And she came skipping back, tail held high, and sat at my feet. I rested my hand on her head and she looked up at me, leaning her head against my knee.

'Come on, mongrel, the kettle will have boiled,' and we ran, side by side, back to the house.

Further Reading

The following is by no means an exhaustive list of books on the much-loved subject of dogs. Some are scholarly, some are historical accounts, some are novels. All are on my bookshelf.

On History, Behaviour and Cognition:

Bradshaw, John, *Dog Sense: How the New Science of Dog Behavior Can Make You a Better Friend to Your Pet* (New York: Basic Books, 2011)

Bradshaw, John, *In Defence of Dogs: Why Dogs Need our Understanding* (London: Allen Lane, 2011)

Coppinger, Raymond and Lorna, *Dog: A New Understanding of Canine Origin, Behavior & Evolution* (Chicago: University of Chicago Press, 2002)

Coren, Stanley, *The Intelligence of Dogs: Canine Consciousness and Capabilities* (New York: The Free Press, 1994)

Fogle, Bruce, *Dog: The Definitive Book for Dog Lovers* (London: Mitchell Beazley, 2010)

Hare, Brian and Woods, Vanessa, *The Genius of Dogs: Discovering the Unique Intelligence of Man's Best Friend* (London: Oneworld Publications, 2014)

Horowitz, Alexandra, *Inside of a Dog: What Dogs See, Smell and Know* (New York: Scribner, 2009)

Miklósi, Ádám, *Dog Behaviour, Evolution and Cognition, Second Edition* (Oxford: Oxford University Press, 2015)

Pickeral, Tamsin, *The Dog: 5000 Years of the Dog in Art* (London: Merrell Publishers, 2008)

Shipman, Pat, *The Invaders: How Humans and Their Dogs Drove Neanderthals to Extinction* (Boston: Harvard University Press, 2015)

On the Ice:

Salisbury, Gay and Laney, *The Cruellest Miles: The Heroic Story of Dogs and Men in a Race Against an Epidemic* (London: Bloomsbury, 2003)

Fiennes, Ranulph, *Captain Scott* (London: Hodder & Stoughton, 2003)

Cherry-Garrard, Apsley, *The Worst Journey in the World* (London: Constable and Co., 1922)

Jones, Hwfa, *The Doggy Men* (Wirrall: Hwfa Jones, 2009)

Ponting, Herbert G. *The Great White South, or, With Scott in the Antarctic* (London: Duckworth, 1921)

Walton, Kevin and Atkinson, Rick, *Of Dogs and Men: Fifty Years in the Antarctic: The Illustrated Story of the Dogs of the British Antarctic Survey 1944–1994* (Worcestershire: Images Publishing (Malvern) Ltd, 1996)

Wheeler, Sara, *Terra Incognita: Travels in Antarctica* (London: Jonathan Cape Ltd, 1996)

At War:

Cooper, Jilly, *Animals at War* (London: Corgi, 1984)

Frankel, Rebecca, *War Dogs: Tales of Canine Heroism, History and Love* (London: Palgrave Macmillan, 2014)

Working Dogs:

Drabble, Phil, *Of Pedigree Unknown: Sporting and Working Dogs* (London: Michael Joseph Ltd, 1976)

Drabble, Phil, *One Man and His Dog* (London: Pelham Books Ltd, 1989)

Some Others I Like:

Fogle, Bruce *Travels with Macy* (London: Ebury Press, 2005)

Rowlands, Mark, *The philosopher and the Wolf: Lessons from the Wild on Love, Death and Happiness* (London: Granta Books, 2008)

Garth Stein, *The Art of Racing in the Rain* (London: HarperCollins, 2009)

Steinbeck, John, *Travels with Charley: In Search of America* (New York: The Viking Press, 1962)

Acknowledgements

Writing a book is a solitary, often selfish, occupation that nonetheless takes the goodwill, patience, advice and timely bottle-opening skills of a great many people. I would firstly like to thank all the people who gave up their time to be interviewed for this book, and the many people who helped set up and arrange interviews and meetings, including Tim Radford, Beccy Hurt, Jenny Moir, Suzanne Ruby, Anne Mills, Amelisa Wright and Raquel Toniolo.

Huge thanks to the people who gave me bolt-holes to escape to at times of panic: Kirsty and James Abel for their kitchen table, spicy soup and restorative glasses of wine at the end of the day; Tim and Pam Fogg for their Bristol flat, as well as wonderful memories of Antarctica; Ian and Jane Jones and family for having me to stay on their farm in Mid Wales and Caroline MacDonald of Blaentrothy Cottages.

For general life-saving services at various times during the writing process thanks to Tim and Sarah Stephens, Rachael Geddes, Nicola Francois, Emily Ryder, Jessica Nock, Rob and Amber Sullivan, Polly Morland, Ophelia Hogan, and Mum and Dad.

Rosemary Scoular is my agent, whose great good sense,

wisdom, advice and encouragement I appreciate more than I can articulate.

Sarah Emsley at Headline first took this project on, and when a far more important project came along – the birth of her daughter Mackenzie – left me in the very lovely and capable hands of Rachel Kenny and Emma Tait. Thank you all.

Living with someone writing a book is absolutely no fun at all. Yet remarkably Ludo stuck around. I don't know why, but I'm jolly glad you did. Woof.

Picture Credits

Find Out More About Kate

www.katehumble.com
www.humblebynature.com
@katehumble

Index

Page numbers in *italic* refer to photographs

Humble by Nature

In 2007, after twenty years of living in London, Kate Humble and her husband Ludo decided it was time to leave city life behind them. Three years later, now the owner of a Welsh smallholding, Kate hears that a nearby farm is to be broken up and sold off. Another farm lost; another opportunity for a young farmless farmer gone. Desperate to stop the sale, Kate contacts the council with an alternative plan – to keep the farm working and to run a rural skills and animal husbandry school alongside it. Against all odds, she succeeds.

In *Humble by Nature*, Kate shares with us a highly personal account of her journey from London town house to Welsh farm. Along the way we meet Bertie and Lawrence the donkeys, Myfanwy and Blackberry the pigs and goats Biscuit and Honey, not forgetting a dog called Badger and his unladylike sidekick Bella. And we are introduced to the tenant farmers Tim and Sarah, the locals who helped and some who didn't, and a whole host of newborn lambs.

Full of the warmth and passion for the natural world that makes Kate such a sought after presenter, *Humble by Nature* is the story of two people prepared to follow their hearts and save a small part of Britain's farming heritage, whatever the consequences.

'You'd have to have a heart of stone not to be touched by Kate's enthusiasm for her new way of life.' *Daily Mail*